Sexuality, Gender, and Policy

Also from Westphalia Press
westphaliapress.org

Sexuality, Gender, and Policy

Vol. 1, No. 1, Fall 2017

Guillermo de los Reyes
Editor

WESTPHALIA PRESS
An imprint of Policy Studies Organization

Sexuality, Gender, and Policy: Vol. 1, No. 1, Fall 2017

Westphalia Press
An imprint of Policy Studies Organization
1527 New Hampshire Ave., NW
Washington, D.C. 20036
info@ipsonet.org

ISBN-13: 978-1-63391-646-3
ISBN-10: 1-63391-646-4

Cover and interior design by Jeffrey Barnes:
jbarnesbook.design

Daniel Gutierrez-Sandoval, Executive Director
PSO and Westphalia Press

Updated material and comments on this edition
can be found at the Westphalia Press website:
www.westphaliapress.org

Sexuality, Gender, and Policy

Vol. 1, No. 1 / Fall 2017

©2017 Policy Studies Organization

Editor's Note

It is my honor to present the first issue of *Sexuality, Gender, and Policy*. SGP will be an open-access and peer-reviewed journal from the Policy Studies Organization that focuses on the social, political, and cultural dimensions of sexuality. Other related policy research, such as that into sexual health, sexual rights, transgender studies, the intersections between disability and queerness, and sexuality education will also find itself represented within these pages. I am incredibly excited by the international reach that this journal will have, and am excited to share our first submissions in this inaugural volume.

At its core, SGP seeks to explore the political processes that have led to the creation and evolution of gender- and sexuality-related policies throughout the world. This means exploring the historical and contemporary methods, theories, topics, and debates that have shaped these fields, while also taking care to account for historical inequalities, marginalization, and post-coloniality.

The specific form of this research will be through the publishing of articles, reviews, syllabi, conference announcements, interviews, panel discussions, and other scholarly insights. We accept the submission of traditional long-form research articles (up to 7,000 words), shorter research notes (of up to 4,000 words), and reviews (of up to 1,000 words), in addition to shorter works.

In the early stages of this journal, we want to celebrate and thank the contributors who have helped to make this inaugural issue possible. The article, "The admission of Lesbians and Gay asylum seekers to the USA: From Victory (ejusdem generis) to Complications (social visibility)" by Tim Braimah proposes that the social visibility test should be rejected by all US courts, and the ejusdem generis approach should be the only adopted test in interpreting membership in a particular social group, and used to adjudge refugee claims based on sexual orientation. Ingrid Holme in her article "Sperm exchange on the black-market; exploring informal sperm-donation through online advertisements" analyses the circumvention of such control, through examining informal sperm donation occurring outside of state regulation. Hole argues that despite official efforts to sanitize the process, the practice of sperm donation is characterized in some quarters by efforts to evade or outflank the official restrictions on it. In "A Study in LGBTQ Activism in Serbia and Russia after 1991: Different Countries, Common Issues?", *Dordevic Vladimir* explores the issue of LGBTQ Activism in Serbia and Russia after 1991. The author discusses whether the said community has so far had any influence in terms of being a possible "driver" of political and social changes, or it has remained but a mere object rather than subject in social and political life. Kunal Debnath in "LGBT Identity: The Illustration of 'Othering' in India" proposes a theoretical approach to understand certain aspects of the otherness in the case of LGBT. Debnath problematizes the important question of what should be the way of the inclusion of the

LGBT community in the mainstream? Finally, in "There's No Thing as a Whole Story': Storytelling and the Healing of Sexual Violence Survivors Among Women and Girls in Acoliland, Northern Uganda", Seun Bamidele studies the role of storytelling in the healing of sexual violence survivors. Informed by the storytelling discourse, Bamidele argues that constructive storytelling exercises can provide an avenue for survivors of sexual violence to acknowledge trauma, attain healing, build resilience, and counter the violent narrative of the group. However, this study also finds that storytelling as a peace-building tool falls short of transforming gender relations.

In this first issue, we have sought to structure and lay the groundwork for further debate on the fundamental issues of sexuality, gender, and policy. To that end, we have begun by asking three leading questions. How and why is sexuality regulated by the state? What are the other social and political actors playing roles in the formation of gender- and sexuality-related policies? And how and why does sexuality often assume an ideologically polarizing role, and how do the various state and non-state actors hold it in relation to other human rights, social norms, and mores?

Thank you for your interest and your contributions, without which none of this would take shape. I look forward to further issues full of debate and illumination. All my best.

Guillermo de los Reyes, Editor in Chief
Sexuality, Gender, and Policy
Associate Professor, Latin American Culture and Literature
Associate Director, Women's Gender and Sexuality Studies Program
University of Houston

编者按

我很荣幸能推出《性、性别和政策》（*Sexuality, Gender and Policy*，简称SGP）期刊的第一期。SGP将会是政策研究机构（Policy Studies Organization）的开放存取期刊，并聚焦于性（sexuality）在社会、政治和文化方面的维度。其他相关的政策研究也会在本期中予以呈现，例如性健康、性权利、跨性别研究、身心障碍和"酷儿性"（queerness）的交汇，以及性教育。我对期刊即将产生的国际影响力感到十分兴奋，同时我很期待将第一卷第一期的投稿文章分享给大家。

SGP的主要目的是对政治过程进行探索，这些政治过程已导致了全球有关性别和性政策的产生和发展。需要探索的部分包括历史方法和当代方法、理论、话题、以及影响这些领域的辩论。探索过程同时应考虑到历史不平等、边缘化和后殖民性等问题。

具体的研究形式将通过发表文章、评论、教学大纲、会议通知、面谈、小组讨论，以及其他学术见解等予以呈现。我们接受传统的长篇研究文章（多达7000字）、短篇研究报告（多达4000字）、评论（多达1000字），以及篇幅更小的作品。

在本刊创立初期，我们想对帮助发表第一期刊物的投稿者表示庆祝和感谢。在文章《允许男女同性恋到美国寻求政治庇护：从胜利（同类规则）到复杂（社会能见度）》中，作者Tim Braimah提出论点，认为"社会能见度测验"（social visibility test）应被一切美国法院拒绝，同时仅采用"同类规则"（ejusdem generis）方法来诠释特定社会团体成员，并在性取向的基础上使用该方法对难民申请（refugee claim）进行裁定。另一篇文章《黑市上的精子交易：对通过网络广告进行非正式捐精的探索》中，作者Ingrid Holme通过检验发生在国家法规之外的非正式精子捐赠，对规避法律控制的行为进行了探索。Holme认为，尽管官方为消除这一过程做出了努力，精子捐赠的实践在某方面来说具有努力逃避或绕开官方对其限制的特征。下一篇文章《关于1991年后塞尔维亚和俄罗斯地区LGBTQ行动主义的研究：不同国家，相同问题？》中，作者Dordevic Vladimir探索了1991年后塞尔维亚和俄罗斯地区LGBTQ行动主义的问题。作者讨论了LGBTQ社区目前是否能产生任何影响，即"驱动"政治和社会变化，还是说社区依然仅是社会和政治生活中的一个客体，而非主体。文章"LGBT认同：印度对'他者'的描述"中，作者Kunal Debnath提出了一项理论方法，用以理解LGBT中"他性"（otherness）的某些方面。Debnath 还提出了一个重要问题，即主流社会应以何种方式接纳LGBT社区？最后一篇文章《所谓的完整故事并不存在：乌干达北部阿乔利人地区的妇女和女孩作为性暴力幸存者讲述她们的治愈过程》中，作者Seun Bamidele研究了"说故事"（storytelling）在治愈性暴力幸存者的过程中扮演的角色。在了解说故事话语之后，Bamidele认为："构造性说故事"（constructive storytelling）能为性暴力幸存者提供一条途径，进而接受创伤、获得治愈、建立忍耐并反抗暴力叙事。然而，此研究还发现，说故事作为一种建立和平的工具却还无法转变性别关系。

在第一期里，我们寻求为今后关于性、性别和政策的重要问题辩论打好基础。为达成这一目标，我们已提出了三个引导性问题。国家如何对性进行管理，这么做的原因是什么？在形成"与性别和性相关的政策"（gender-and sexuality-related policies）过程中，还有哪些社会和政治行为者扮演了角色？性如何时常能承担"思想上的两极分化"（ideologically polarizing）角色，原因是什么；不同国家行为者和非国家行为者如何将性和其他人权以及社会规范等方面联系起来？

感谢大家对本刊的关注和投稿，这一切对期刊而言都是必不可少的。我期待之后的每一期都充满辩论和启迪。献上我最美好的祝愿。

主编Guillermo de los Reyes

《性、性别和政策》

"拉美文化和文学"（Latin American Culture and Literature）副教授

"女性性别和性研究项目"（Women's Gender and Sexuality Studies Program）副主任

休斯顿大学

Es un honor presentar la primera edición de *Sexuality, Gender and Policy*. *SGP* será una revista arbitrada y de libre acceso de la Policy Studies Organization que se enfoca en las dimensiones culturales, políticas y sociales de la sexualidad. Asimismo, otras áreas de estudio relacionadas, como la investigación acerca de la salud sexual, los derechos sexuales, los estudios LGBTQ+, las intersecciones entre la discapacidad y lo *queer* y la educación sexual se encontrará representada en estas páginas. Me emociona enormemente el alcance internacional que tendrá esta revista, y me complace compartir nuestras primeras contribuciones en esta edición inaugural.

En esencia, SGP busca explorar los procesos que han llevado a la creación y evolución de políticas de género y sexualidad a través del mundo. Esto significa explorar métodos históricos y contemporáneos, teorías, temas y debates que han formado estos campos de estudio, mientras se encargan de incluir las inequidades históricas, la marginalización y la postcolonialidad.

La forma específica de esta investigación será a través de la publicación de artículos, reseñas, programas de estudios, anuncios de conferencias, entrevistas, discusiones relevantes y otros conocimientos académicos. Aceptamos la contribución de artículos de investigación de formato largo tradicional (hasta 7000 palabras), notas de investigación más cortas (hasta 4000 palabras) y reseñas (hasta 1000 palabras), y también de otros trabajos más pequeños.

En las etapas tempranas de esta revista, queremos celebrar y agradecer a los contribuyentes que han ayudado a hacer posible la elaboración de esta primera edición. El artículo, "The admission of Lesbians and Gay asylum seekers to the USA: From Victory (ejusdem generis) to Complications (social visibility)" de Tim Braimah sugiere que la prueba de visibilidad social debería ser rechazada por todas las cortes de los Estados Unidos y que la aproximación *ejusdem generis* debería ser la única prueba adoptada para interpretar la pertenencia a un grupo social, y utilizada para procesar las solicitudes de asilo que se basan en la orientación sexual. Ingrid Holme, en su artículo "Sperm exchange on the black-market; exploring informal sperm-donation through online advertisements," analiza la circunvención de este control al examinar la donación informal de esperma que ocurre fuera de las leyes del estado. Holme argumenta que a pesar de los esfuerzos oficiales para limpiar el proceso, la práctica de donación de esperma está caracterizada en algunos ámbitos por esfuerzos para evadir o salirse de las restricciones oficiales. En "A Study in LGBTQ Activism in Serbia and Russia after 1991: Different Countries, Common Issues?," Batueva Ekaterina y Dordevic Vladimir exploran el tema del activismo LGBTQ en Serbia y Rusia después de 1991. Los autores analizan si la comunidad mencionada ha tenido hasta este punto influencia en términos de ser un "conductor" posible de cambios políticos y sociales o si ha permanecido como un simple objeto y no un sujeto en la vida social y política. Kunal Debnath en "LGBT Identity: The Illustration of 'Othering' in India" propone una aproximación teórica para comprender ciertos aspectos de la otredad en el caso de la comunidad LGBT. Debnath problematiza la importante pregunta de cuál debería ser la forma de inclusión de la comunidad LGBT en la sociedad en general. Finalmente, en "There's No Thing as a Whole Story': Storytelling and the Healing of Sexual Violence Survivors Among Women and Girls in Acoliland, Northern Uganda," Seun Bamidele estudia el rol del discurso en forma de narración de historias para la sanación de los sobrevivientes de violencia sexual. Informado por el discurso en forma de narración de historias, Bamidele argumenta que los ejercicios constructivos de narración pueden proporcionar una vía para que los sobrevivientes de violencia sexual reconozcan el trauma, obtengan sanación, desarrollen resiliencia, y contrarresten la narrativa violenta del grupo. Sin embargo, este estudio también encuentra que la narración de historias como herramienta de construcción de paz no llega completamente a transformar las relaciones de género.

En esta primera edición, hemos buscado estructurar y construir las bases para un debate más profundo acerca de los problemas fundamentales de la sexualidad, el género y la política pública. Para este propósito, hemos empezado por hacer tres preguntas tendenciosas. ¿Cómo y por qué el estado regula la sexualidad? ¿Cuáles son otros actores sociales y políticos que juegan un papel en la formación de políticas de género y sexualidad? ¿Y cómo y por qué la sexualidad a menudo asume un papel ideológicamente polarizador, y cómo los diferentes actores estatales y no-estatales lo mantienen en relación con otros derechos humanos, normas sociales, y costumbres?

Gracias por su interés y sus contribuciones, sin las cuales nada de esto podría tomar forma. Espero que haya ediciones futuras llenas de debate e iluminación. Mis mejores deseos.

Guillermo de los Reyes, Editor Principal
Sexuality, Gender and Policy
Profesor Asociado, Cultura y literatura Latinoamericana
Director Asociado, Women's Gender and Sexuality Studies Program
Universidad de Houston

The Admission of Lesbians and Gay Asylum Seekers to the USA: From Victory (Ejusdem Generis) to Complications (Social Visibility)

Tim S. Braimah
University of Huddersfield, United Kingdom

Abstract

Under US asylum law, lesbians and gay men are considered members of a particular social group as established by the case of Toboso-Alfonso. The phrase "membership in a particular social group" was effectively defined in Matter of Acosta, based on the doctrine of ejusdem generis. The ejusdem generis approach was utilized until 2006, when the Board of Immigration Appeal (BIA) introduced a new interpretation of membership in a particular social group, known as the social visibility test, which requires lesbians and gay men to be visible and recognizable in their societies to be eligible for asylum. Unlike the BIA's social visibility test, the ejusdem generis approach grants asylum to lesbians and gay men on the basis that their sexuality is innate and fundamental to their identity. This article presents arguments to suggest that the social visibility test should be rejected by all US courts, and the ejusdem generis approach should be the only adopted test in interpreting membership in a particular social group, and used to adjudge refugee claims based on sexual orientation.

Keywords: Membership of a Particular Social Group, Sexual Orientation, Same-Sex Refugees, Social Visibility, Ejusdem Generis, US Asylum, Matter of Acosta

摘要

在美国庇护法下，女同性恋者和男同性恋者被视为特定社会团体成员—该团体的成立源于Toboso-Alfonso案件（the case of Toboso-Alfonso）。基于同类规则（ejusdem generis）学说，"特定社会团体成员资格"这一说法在Acosta事件（Matter of

Acosta）中得出了有效定义。同类规则方法一直到2006年还在使用，当时移民上诉委员会（简称BIA）对特定社会团体成员资格进行了新的诠释，将其称之为"社会能见度测验（"会能cial visibility test），它要求男女同性恋者需在社会上受到认可才能有资格寻求庇护。与BIA的社会能见度测验不同的是，同类规则方法认为男女同性恋者的性取向是天生的，取向对其自身认同十分重要，并在此基础上给予庇护。本文提出论点，认为社会能见度测验应被一切美国法院拒绝，同时仅采用同类规则方法来诠释特定社会团体成员，并在性取向的基础上使用该方法裁定难民的合法权利。

关键词：特定社会团体成员资格；性取向；同性难民；社会能见度；同类规则；美国避难；Matter of Acosta

Resumen

Bajo la ley de asilo en Estados Unidos, las lesbianas y los homosexuales son considerados miembros de un grupo social particular, tal como se estableció en el caso Toboso-Alfonso. La frase "afiliación a un grupo social particular" fue definida de manera efectiva en Matter of Acosta, basado en la doctrina de *eiusdem generis*. El enfoque de *eiusdem generis* fue utilizado hasta 2006, cuando el BIA (Board of Immigration Appeal-Junta de Apelaciones de Inmigración) introdujo una nueva interpretación de afiliación en un grupo social particular, conocido como el examen de visibilidad social, el cual requiere que las lesbianas y los homosexuales sean visibles e identificables en sus sociedades para ser elegidos para el asilo. A diferencia del examen de visibilidad social del BIA, el enfoque *eiusdem generis* otorga asilo a las lesbianas y los homosexuales bajo las bases de que su sexualidad es innata y fundamental para su identidad. En el siguiente artículo se presentan argumentos que proponen que el examen de visibilidad social debería rechazarse en todas las cortes de Estados Unidos, y en su lugar, debería optarse por el enfoque *eiusdem generis* como interpretación única de "afiliación a un grupo social particular"; y usado para adjudicar las demandas basadas en orientación sexual.

Palabras clave: *Miembro de un grupo social particular, orientación sexual, refugiados del mismo sexo, visibilidad social, eiusdem generis, asilo en Estados Unidos, Matter of Acosta.*

Introduction

While lesbians and gay men fleeing persecution from their homelands can currently find refuge in the United States, historically this was not always the case. For most of the history of the United States, same-sexuality[1] has been a crime, and lesbians and gay men have been categorized as persons afflicted with a mental disorder. However, in 1973, the American Psychiatric Association (APA) removed same-sexuality from its list of mental disorders. The normalization of same-sexuality by the APA arguably created the opportunity for lesbians and gay men fleeing persecution to claim asylum in the United States.

Since the 1980s, the United States has been awarding refugee claims based on sexual orientation despite the fact that the US Refugee Act of 1980 does not explicitly mention sexual orientation as grounds for persecution in its refugee definition.[2] It has relied on the definition "membership of a particular social group" in dealing with refugee claims based on sexual orientation. The US courts interpreted the phrase "membership in a particular social group" as

Matter of Acosta,[3] based on the canon of construction, *ejusdem generis*. Under the *Matter of Acosta* approach, lesbians and gay men are granted asylum on the basis that their same-sexuality is innate and fundamental to their identity. However, the *Matter of Acosta* approach was utilized until 2006, when the Board of Immigration Appeal (BIA) introduced a new interpretation of "membership of a particular social group," known as the Social Visibility test. Applying the approach to sexual orientation claims, the test only recognizes lesbians and gay men who have characteristics which would be demonstrably recognizable in their native country. In this article, I argue that the Social Visibility doctrine should be rejected by all US courts, and the *Matter of Acosta*[4] approach should remain the only interpretation of membership of a particular social group, while dealing with refugee claims based on sexual orientation.

Part II of this article begins by discussing the historical treatment of lesbians and gay men in US Immigration Law. The article exposes how the removal of same-sexuality as a mental disorder by the APA led to a gateway for refugee claims based on sexual orienta-

---

1   I use the term same-sexuality to refer to the sexuality of lesbians and gay men, as opposed to homosexuality, as the latter terminology is clinical.

2   U.S Refugee Act of 1980: Public Law No. 96-212, 94 Stat. 102 (1980) (defines a refugee as "any person who is outside any country of such person's nationality or, in the case of a person having no nationality, is outside any country in which such a person last habitually resided, and who is unable or unwilling to return to, and who is unable or unwilling to avail himself or herself of the protection of that country because of persecution or a well- founded fear of persecution on account of race, religion, nationality, membership in a particular social group, or political opinion"). The US definition of refugee was transplanted from the 1951 Geneva Convention Relating to the Status of Refugees and the 1967 Protocol:

3   *See* 19 I&N, December 211, 232 (Board of Immigration Appeal 1985.).

4   19 I&N Dec. 211, 232 (BIA 1985).

tion in the United States. In Part III, I discuss two ground-breaking asylum cases in US asylum law, namely *Matter of Acosta*[5] and *Toboso-Alfonso*.[6] I present the importance of these two cases in US asylum law in relation to the definition of membership in a particular social group, and the establishment of lesbians and gay men as a particular social group under US asylum law. Part IV discusses the Social Visibility doctrine, used to interpret membership of a particular social group. In this section, academic debates and the impact the Social Visibility test would have in deciding refugee claims based on sexual orientation are presented. Part V presents conclusions and provides reasons why the social visibility test should be rejected, and why the *Matter of Acosta* interpretation of a particular social group should be the only interpretation adopted while dealing with refugee claims based on sexual orientation.

PART II

Historical Treatment of Lesbians and Gay Men in US Immigration Law

The United States acceded to the 1967 Protocol Relating to the Status of Refugees on No-vember 1, 1968.[7] As a signatory to the 1967 Protocol, the United States affords refuge to those fleeing persecution on the basis of race, religion, nationality, and membership in a particular social group, or political opinion. Histori-cally, same-sex-oriented persons seek-ing refugee status were excluded from entering the United States because same-sexuality was considered a men-tal disorder. Section 9 of the immigra-tion Act of 1917 stated that:

> [I]t shall be unlawful for any person, including any transpor-tation company other than rail-way lines entering the USA from foreign contiguous ter-ritory, or the owner, master, agent, or consignee of any vessel to bring to the USA either from a foreign country or any insu-lar possession of the USA any alien afflicted with idiocy, in-sanity, imbecility, feeble-mind-edness, epilepsy, constitutional psychopathic inferiority, chronic alcoholism, tuberculosis in any form, or a loathsome or danger-ous contagious disease.[8]

This meant that same-sex-ori-ented persons, who at that time were considered mentally ill, were excluded from entering the United States. The situation of same-sex-oriented persons

---

5   *Ibid.*

6   *See* Matter of Toboso-Alfonso, 20 I. & N. Dec 819 (BIA 1990).

7   Though the USA is a signatory to the 1967 Protocol, it did not sign the 1951 Convention Relating to the Status of Refugees.

8   U.S Department of Labor: Bureau of Immigration. Immigration Laws, Rules of May 1, 1917. Washington Government Printing Office 1920, 10.

wishing to enter the United States did not change even when, in 1952, Congress changed the Immigration and Nationality Act. The 1952 Immigration and Nationality Act prohibited same-sex- oriented persons from entering the United States on the basis that they were afflicted with a psychopathic personality or a mental disorder.[9]

The first major same-sex-oriented case which addressed the phrase "psychopathic personality" in the United States was the case of *USA v. Flores-Rodriguez*.[10] In that case, Flores-Rodriguez had been convicted of perjury for failing to disclose in an application for an immigrant visa that he had been convicted of loitering in a public place for the purpose of soliciting men. On appeal, Florez-Rodriguez stated that even if he had disclosed his conviction it would not have affected his visa application under the then existing law.

However, the Court of Appeal disagreed and held that, on the basis of the 1917 Immigration Act (which was currently in force), he (Flores-Rodriguez) could have been barred either as a person of constitutionally psychopathic inferiority or as a mentally defective individual. Despite the failure by the government to present evidence

that same-sex-oriented people were included in the category of constitutional psychopathic inferiority, it was concluded by the court that Flores-Rodriguez's professed same-sex orientation and conviction were enough to put him in the psychopathic category.[11]

Furthermore, in the early 1960s, same-sex-oriented persons in the United States were constantly treated unfairly, particularly by the courts. In certain cases, the courts refused to consider appeals of rulings concerning same-sex-oriented persons who were to be deported. For example, in the case of *Quiroz v. Neely*,[12] a Mexican woman was found to be afflicted with a psychopathic personality based upon evidence of her same-sex orientation. Despite statements by doctors that same-sex orientation was not considered a mental disorder by the medical profession, the 5th Circuit upheld the deportation in *Quiroz v. Neely*.[13] The Court of Appeal of the 5th Circuit found the description "psychopathic" applicable to same-sex-oriented persons. The court concluded that from the Act's legislative history, although the phrase "psychopathic personality" may mean a different thing entirely to psychiatrists, for the Congress's purposes, it was intended to include same-sex-oriented

---

9   Joan Burda, *Gay, Lesbian and Transgender Clients: A Lawyers Guide* (New York: American Bar Association, 2008), 247.

10   237 F.2d 405 (1956).

11   See Carro Jorge, "From Constitutional Psychopathic Inferiority to Aids: What is in the Future for Homosexual Alien's Overview: Domestic Implications of Immigration Policy," *Yale Law and Policy Review* 7 (1989): 210. [Hereinafter *From Constitutional Psychopathic Inferiority to Aids*].

12   Quiroz v. Nelly, 291 F.2d 906 (5th Cir. 1961).

13   *Ibid.*

persons. [14] However, within a year, the court reached conflicting decisions when it ruled in *Fleuti v. Rosenberg*[15] that a Swiss gay man would not be excluded or deported from the United States. In *Fleuti v. Rosenberg,* [16] the defendant was admitted lawfully to the United States on October 9, 1952 for permanent residence. He remained in the United States until 1956, until he travelled to Mexico for a couple of hours on August 25, 1956. Three years later, in April 1959, the Immigration and Naturalization service sought to deport Fleuti on the grounds that at the time of his return from Mexico in 1956, he was an alien afflicted with psychopathic personality based on evidence of his same-sex activities. Therefore he was within one or more of the classes of aliens excluded from the United States under the 1952 Immigration and Nationality Act. However, the Court of Appeal for the 9th Circuit cancelled the deportation order, holding that the term "psychopathic personality" was unconstitutionally vague in that it did not sufficiently encompass same-sexuality. In addition, as the term "psychopathic personality" was not defined in the statute, it was held by the 9th Circuit that the case against Fleuti was void for

vagueness. According to the vagueness doctrine, the due process of statute is violated if its language fails to provide comprehensible warnings about proscribed conduct.[17]

In the same year as the case of *Fleuti v. Rosenberg,* [18] the vagueness doctrine was invoked in the case of *Lavoie v. Immigration and Naturalization Service.*[19] The case of *Lavoie v. Immigration and Naturalization Service*[20] involved the overturning of the deportation of a permanent resident from Canada who had pleaded guilty to a charge of lewd and indecent behavior. In 1965, as a result of the 9th Circuit decision in *Fleuti v. Rosenberg,*[21] the US Congress, in order to avoid any confusion as to whether the term "psychopathic personality" included same-sexuality, amended the Immigration and Nationality Act by adding "sexual deviation," clarifying that same-sex-oriented persons were barred from entering the United States. Nonetheless, as confusion still surrounded the phrase "psychopathic personality," in order to exclude same-sex-oriented persons from the United States, the USA Supreme Court sought to clarify the law in *Boutilier v. Immigration and Naturalization Ser-*

---

14   *From Constitutional Psychopathic Inferiority to Aids, supra* note 3.

15   Fleuti v. Rosenberg, 302 F.2d 652 (9th Cir. 1962), vacated and remanded on other grounds, 374 US 449 (1963).

16   *Ibid.*

17   *Ibid.*

18   *Supra* note 14.

19   *Supra* note 21.

20   *Ibid.*

21   *Supra* note 14.

vice.[22] As a result, the Supreme Court wrestled with four questions in *Boutilier v. Immigration and Naturalization Service.*[23] First, did Congress intend to exclude and deport all same-sex-oriented aliens through the psychopathic personality provisions of the 1952 Immigration and Nationality Act? Second, did the Act's Public Health Service certification procedure require medical authorities to defer to legal definitions or legal authorities to defer to medical definitions? Third, was the phrase "afflicted with psychopathic personality" unconstitutionally vague? Fourth and lastly, were aliens to be classified as afflicted with psychopathic personality on the basis of same-sex conduct or character?[24]

In the case of *Boutilier v. Immigration and Naturalization Service*,[25] despite evidence of the petitioner's same-sex orientation, and his admission that he had once been arrested for same-sex activity, the special inquiry officer ordered Boutilier to be deported based on the fact he had been gay at the time of his entry into America and thus was to be excluded as one afflicted with a psychopathic personality.[26] The decision in *Boutilier v. Immigration and*

Naturalization Service[27] finally clarified that same-sex-oriented persons could not be admitted to the United States. Despite the linkage of same-sexuality to psychopathic personalities, in 1973, the American Psychiatric Association removed same-sex orientation from its list of mental disorders. After the dropping of same-sex orientation from the list of mental disorders, the then president of the American Psychiatrist Association, John P. Spiegel, urged the Immigration and Naturalization Service to use their statutory powers to refrain from excluding, deporting, or refusing citizenship to same-sex-oriented persons.[28] The response by the Immigration and Naturalization Service counsel was that the 1965 statute and the decision in *Boutilier v. Immigration and Naturalization Service*[29] made such a change impossible.[30]

In November 1979, the Public Health Service announced that it could no longer issue Class A certificates declaring that same-sex-oriented persons had a mental disorder. According to Eskridge, the announcement threw the statutory scheme into turmoil because a Class A certificate was needed in order to exclude or deport

---

22 *Supra* note 21.

23 *Ibid.*

24 Supreme Court's decisions from Griswold to Roe, 61, (University of North Carolina).

25 *Supra* note 21.

26 *From Constitutional Psychopathic Inferiority to Aids, supra* note 3.

27 *Supra* note 21.

28 William Eskridge, *Gaylaw: Challenging The Apartheid of the Closet* (England: Harvard University, 2009), 133.

29 *Supra* note 21.

30 Ibid., 133.

same-sex-oriented people from the United States. Nevertheless, despite the Public Health Service decision, the Office of the Legal Counsel advised the Immigration and Naturalization Service that it was required to enforce the decision in *Boutilier v. Immigration and Naturalization Service*[31] even without the co-operation of the Public Health Service.[32]

Heeding this advice, the Immigration and Naturalization Service introduced a new procedure to inspect aliens who were suspected of being same-sex oriented. Under the new procedure, unless an arriving same-sex-oriented person made an "unambiguous oral or written admission of same-sex orientation" or a third person arriving at the same time "voluntarily stated," without prompting or prior questioning, that an alien who arrived in the United States at the same time was same-sex oriented, the alien would not be questioned about his or her sexual preference. If, however, the arriving alien volunteered the information or a third party arriving at the same time identified the alien as same-sex oriented, the alien would be excludable.[33]

The importance of the Public Health Service Class A certificates and the policy of the Immigration and Naturalization Service were soon to be tested in the case of *Hill v. Immigration and Naturalization Service*.[34] In that case, Carl Hill wanted to enter the United States as a non-immigrant visitor. Because he had made an unsolicited statement at the port of entry that he was gay, he was detained by the Immigration and Nationality Service. But he later secured a temporary restraining order and was paroled into the country.[35] However, Carl Hill was subjected to an exclusion hearing to decide whether he was to be excluded from the United States. At the exclusion hearing, the Immigration and Naturalization Service found themselves in a dilemma when the immigration judge ruled that Carl Hill was not excludable from the United States because the government could not present a medical certificate from the Public Health Service stating that he was psychopathic as a result of his same-sex orientation. The Court further reasoned that if same-sex orientation was no longer considered an illness by the medical profession, applying *Boutilier v. Immigration and Naturalization Service*[36] and excluding same-sex-oriented persons from the United States was no longer the law.[37]

---

31 *Supra* note 21.

32 Eskridge, *Gaylaw*.

33 *From Constitutional Psychopathic Inferiority to Aids, supra* note 3.

34 714 F.2d 1470 Hill v. Immigration and Naturalization Service, 714 (F.2D 1470).

35 Margarot Canaday, *The Straight State: Sexuality and Citizenship in 20ᵗʰ Century America* (Princeton, NJ: Princeton University, 2011), 250.

36 *Supra* note 23.

37 *From Constitutional Psychopathic Inferiority to Aids, supra* note 3.

However, despite the 9th Circuit decision that the US government could only exclude same-sex-oriented persons with a Class A certificate issued by the Public Health Service, the 9th Circuit reached a different decision in *re Longstaff*[38] when it held that a resident alien who had lived in the United States for 15 years was unlawfully admitted because while entering the United States, he was same-sex oriented, and therefore excludable as a person afflicted with mental illness.[39]

The differing decisions in the cases above illuminate the differing attitudes toward same-sexuality in the United States during that period. While the 1952 Immigration and Nationality Act excluded same-sex-oriented persons from entering the United States because they were afflicted with psychopathic personalities, the medical profession held that there was no evidence to prove that same-sex-oriented persons had mental defects. These different opinions created problems for same-sex-oriented persons fleeing persecution and migrating to the United States as exemplified in the cases above. In addition, the exclusion of same-sex-oriented persons remained in

force in the USA until 1990. However, to conform to the medical profession's assertion that same-sexuality was not a mental defect, Congress introduced the Immigration Act of 1990. This eliminated sections of the 1952 Immigration and Nationality Act, which had been used to exclude same-sex-oriented persons from the USA as suffering from mental defects. According to Park Jin, after the 1990 Immigration Act eliminated the exclusion of same-sex-oriented persons from the USA, three same-sex-oriented persons[40] brought refugee claims on the grounds that they constituted members of a particular social group.[41] Furthermore, although the USA had dealt with refugee claims on the basis of sexual orientation during the 1950s and 1960s, and was a signatory to the 1967 Protocol, the term "refugee" was first legally defined in the 1980 Refugee Act. The Refugee Act of 1980 contained a similar definition of a refugee in the 1951 Refugee Convention and the 1967 Protocol. In addition, as Mahler maintains, the main reason the United States adopted the 1980 Refugee Act was to conform to international law and show the United States's commitment to in-

---

38 Longstaffe v. Immigration and Naturalization Service, 716 F.2d 1439 (5th Cir. 1983).

39 Marc Stein, *Gay, Lesbian and Transgender Clients: A Lawyers Guide* (Cengage: American Bar Association, 2004), 248.

40 See: Pitcherskaia v Immigration and Naturalization Service (Russian lesbian living in San Francisco who suffered repeated arrests and physical violence while living in Russia); A.T. (Iranian gay man who feared persecution if he returned to his country); Jacobo Rivas (Nicaraguan gay man who feared persecution if he returned to his country based on the fact he had Aids and was same-sex oriented).

41 Park Jin, Pink Asylum: Political Asylum Eligibility of Gay men and Lesbians under US immigration Policy, University of California Law Review 42 (1994–1995).

ternational humanitarian principles.[42] Although the 1980 Refugee Act contained a similar definition to those of the 1951 Refugee Convention and the 1967 Protocol, like the drafters of the Refugee Convention, the US Congress gave no indication as to how the term "membership of a particular group" should be interpreted. Nevertheless, the definition and interpretation of "membership of a particular social group" was to change in the landmark case of *Matter of Acosta*.[43]

PART III

Matter of Acosta: Groundbreaking Asylum Jurisprudence

In *Matter of Acosta*,[44] the US BIA held as follows:

> We find the well-established doctrine of *ejusdem generis*, meaning literally, "of the same kind to be most helpful in constructing the phrase" membership of a particular social group. That doctrine holds that general words used in an enumeration with specific words should be construed in a manner consistent with specific words. The other grounds of persecution in

the Act and the Protocol listed in association with "membership in a particular social group" are persecution on account of "race," "religion," "nationality," and "political opinion." Each of these grounds describes persecution aimed at an immutable characteristic: a characteristic that either is beyond the power of an individual to change or is so fundamental to individual identity or conscience that it ought not to be required to be changed.[45]

In *Matter of Acosta*,[46] the claimant based his refugee claim on persecution that he had suffered due to his membership of a particular social group, namely "COTAXI drivers and persons involved in the transportation industry in El Salvador." Denying Acosta's asylum claim, the BIA determined that taxi drivers in El Salvador did not possess an "immutable characteristic" because group members could avoid threat from guerrillas by either changing jobs or cooperating in work stoppages.[47] This decision solidified the interpretation of membership of a particular social group as the possession of an immutable or innate characteristic that cannot be changed. Unlike sex or color, Acosta's profession could easily

---

42 Sarah Mahler, *American Dream: Immigrant Life on the Margins* (Princeton, NJ: Princeton University Press, 1995), 175.

43 *See* 19 I&N December 211, 232 (Board of Immigration Appeal 1985).

44 *Ibid.*

45 *Matter of Acosta*, A-24159781, USABoard of Immigration Appeals, March 1, 1985, http://www.unhcr.org/refworld/docid/3ae6b6b910.html (accessed August 17, 2012).

46 *Ibid.*

47 *Ibid.*

be changed in order to avoid persecution. In addition, under the immutability test explained in *Matter of Acosta*,[48] three possible categories which an individual may claim as membership of a particular social group were identified:

1. Groups defined by an innate or unalterable characteristic;

2. Groups whose members voluntarily associate for reasons fundamental to their human dignity that they should not be forced to forsake the association; and

3. Groups associated by a former voluntary status, unalterable due to its historic permanence.[49]

Furthermore, despite the interpretative guidance on membership of a particular social group by the BIA, the 9th Circuits court adopted a different definition of "particular social group" in *Sanchez-Trujillo v. Immigration and Naturalization Service*.[50] The 9th Circuit's decision in *Sanchez-Trujillo v. Immigration and Naturalization Service*[51] that a group of young men of military age were not members of a particular social group and as a result did not qualify for refugee status and, disregarding the Board of Immigration guidance in *Matter of Acosta*,[52] stated that:

[A] Particular social group implies a collection of people closely affiliated with each other, who are actuated by some common impulse or interest. Of central concern is the existence of a voluntary associational relationship among the purported members, which imparts some common characteristic that is fundamental to the identity of that Under *Sanchez-Trujillo v. Immigration and Naturalization Service*, the Court established a four step test for persecution on the basis of group membership. These steps included decision being made as to whether the classes of people identified by the petitioners are cognizable as a social group. Petitioners being able to establish that they qualify as members of the group. Determination as to whether the social group has been target for persecution on account of the characteristics of its members. Considerations as to whether such special circumstances are present to warrant in regarding mere membership in that social group as constituting per se eligibility for asylum or prohibition of deportation.[53]

Despite the different interpretation of membership of a particu-

---

48   *Ibid.*

49   James Hathaway, *The Law of Refugee Status* (Toronto: Butterworths, 1991), 161.

50   Sanchez-Trujillo v. Immigration and Naturalization Service, 801 F.2d 1571 (9th Cir. 1986).

51   *Ibid.*

52   *Matter of Acosta*, A-24159781, USABoard of Immigration Appeals, March 1, 1985, http://www.unhcr.org/refworld/docid/3ae6b6b910.html (accessed August 17, 2012).

53   Sanchez-Trujillo v. Immigration and Naturalization Service, 801 F.2d 1571 (9th Cir. 1986).

lar social group by the BIA and the 9th Circuit, other federal circuit courts have largely adopted the BIA interpretation of membership of a particular social group in *Matter of Acosta*. Although the cases of *Sanchez-Trujillo v. Immigration and Naturalization Service*[54] and *Matter of Acosta*[55] provided interpretations of the nebulous Refugee Convention grounds, "membership of a particular social group," both cases did not specifically address whether same-sex-oriented persons constituted a particular social group. However, this was to change in the case of *Matter of Toboso-Alfonso*.[56] The case concerned a gay man from Cuba who arrived in the United States, having fled persecution at the hands of police officials and the Cuban government. In *Matter of Toboso-Alfonso*,[57] the legal representative argued before the immigration judge that his client was a member of a particular social group, namely persecuted same-sex-oriented persons in Cuba. The immigration judge found Toboso-Alfonso's testimony to be credible, and concluded that Toboso-Alfonso had been persecuted and had a well-founded fear of continuous persecution in Cuba, and that Toboso-Alfonso's persecution resulted in his membership of a particular social group,

namely same-sex-oriented persons. Despite this decision, the Immigration and Naturalization Service appealed the case to the BIA, arguing that:

> Socially deviated behavior, i.e. same-sex activity is not a basis for finding a social group within the contemplation of the Act and that such a conclusion "would be tantamount to awarding discretionary relief to those involved in behaviour that is not only socially deviant in nature, but in violation of the laws and regulations of the country as well."[58]

Nonetheless, the BIA dismissed the Immigration and Naturalization Service appeal and granted Toboso-Alfonso asylum on the basis that if he returned to Cuba, he would be persecuted. Reaching the decision in *Matter of Toboso-Alfonso*,[59] the BIA focused on Toboso-Alfonso's same-sex orientation rather than his same-sex activities in Cuba. According to the BIA: "The government's actions against him were not in response to specific conduct on his part (e.g. for engaging in same-sex activities); simply they resulted from his status as being same-sex oriented."[60]

---

54 *Ibid.*

55 *Matter of Acosta*, A-24159781, USA Board of Immigration Appeals, March 1, 1985, http://www.unhcr.org/refworld/docid/3ae6b6b910.html (accessed August 17, 2012).

56 *Matter of Toboso-Alfonso*, USA Board of Immigration Appeals, March 12, 1990, http://www.refworld.org/docid/3ae6b6b84.html (accessed March 12, 2012).

57 *Ibid.*

58 *Ibid.*

59 *Ibid.*

60 *Ibid.*

Matter of Toboso-Alfonso: Same-sex-oriented Persons as "Members of a Particular Social Group"

The ruling in *Matter of Toboso-Al-fonso*[61] was significant because it established same-sex-oriented persons as members of a particular social group. Although the status of a particular social group was defined in *Matter of Acosta*,[62] that case did not extensively clarify whether same-sex-oriented persons were a particular social group, thus it was not fully established that same-sex-oriented persons were a particular social group until the landmark case of *Matter of Toboso-Alfonso*.[63]

Furthermore, the case of *Matter of Toboso-Alfonso*[64] was followed by the case of *Matter of Marcelo Tenorio*.[65] The latter case concerned a 30-year-old gay man from Brazil who was beaten and stabbed at a bus stop in Brazil because he was same-sex oriented. In reaching their decision in *Matter of Marcelo Tenorio*,[66] the courts combined the tests of *Matter of Acosta*[67] and *Sanchez-Trujillo v. Immigration and Naturalization Service*.[68] Based upon the evidence submitted, the court found that Marcelo-Tenorio's fear of persecution on account of his membership of a particular social group was objectively reasonable, and thus a person in Marcelo-Tenorio's position would fear future persecution by anti-gay groups in Brazil.

In 1994, asylum matters concerning same-sex-oriented persons were clarified when Attorney General Janet Reno issued a directive that the US Immigration system adopt *Matter of Toboso-Alfonso*[69] as a precedent in all proceedings involving same-sex issues. Attorney General Janet Reno stated that "an individual who had been identified as same-sex oriented and persecuted by his or her government for that reason alone may be eligible for relief under the refugee laws on the basis of persecution because of membership of a particular social group."[70]

Since *Matter of Toboso-Alfonso*[71] set a precedent for deciding

---

61 *Ibid.*

62 *Ibid.*

63 *Ibid.*

64 *Ibid.*

65 A72 093 558, 9th Circ.

66 *Ibid.*

67 *Matter of Acosta*, A-24159781, USA Board of Immigration Appeals, March 1, 1985, http://www.un-hcr.org/refworld/docid/3ae6b6b910.html (accessed August 17, 2012).

68 *Sanchez-Trujillo, et al., v. Immigration and Naturalization Service*, 801 F.2d 1571, USA Court of Appeals for the Ninth Circuit, October 15, 1986.

69 *Ibid.*

70 Robert Leitner, "Flawed System Exposed: The Immigration Adjudicatory System and Asylum for Sexual Minorities," *University of Miami Law Review* 58 (2004): 687.

71 *Matter of Toboso-Alfonso*, USA Board of Immigration Appeals, March 12, 1990.

same-sex-oriented cases, and *Matter of Acosta*[72] for defining a particular social group as an innate or immutable characteristic, the US Immigration Service have been able to decide cases on refugee claims based on sexual orientation. However, the definition of a particular social group in *Matter of Acosta*[73] remained undisturbed until 2006 when the US BIA introduced the Social Visibility test as an additional requirement in determining whether groups such as same-sex-oriented persons qualified for refugee status. Following the introduction of a new test for determining membership of a particular social group in the United States, Bresnahan states that the confusion surrounding the meaning of a particular social group is now more acute than ever.[74] Bresnahan makes a resounding statement, because the convention ground membership of a particular social group had been made amorphous by the drafters of the Refugee Convention not providing an interpretation or definition for the ground membership of a particular social group. Therefore, the US immigration system made a breakthrough in refugee law by providing a definition and test in *Matter of Acosta*,[75] only to further throw the ground "member-ship of a particular social group" into a more confusing state, by introducing an additional requirement or test (social visibility) for determining membership of a particular social group.

Subsequently, despite creating more obscurity in an already obscure area of law (definition of membership of a particular social group), the United States has at least brought clarification on how to define membership of a particular social group in *Matter of Acosta*.[76] By defining membership of a particular social group in *Matter of Acosta*[77] as an innate and immutable characteristic or a characteristic so fundamentally identifiable that even if changeable, it should not be required to change, the United States set a world precedent in defining membership of a particular social group. Its definition influenced jurisdictions such as Canada and the UK's interpretation of membership in a particular social group.[78]

PART IV

While the United States had made such progress with *Matter of Acosta's*[79] interpretation of a particular social group, the

---

72   *Matter of Acosta*, A-24159781, USA Board of Immigration Appeals, March 1, 1985.

73   *Ibid.*

74   Kristin Bresnahan, "The Board of Immigration Appeals's New "Social Visibility" Test for Determining "Membership of a Particular Social Group in Asylum Claims and Its Legal and Policy Implications," *Berkeley Journal of International Law* 649–679 (2011).

75   *Matter of Acosta*, A-24159781, USA Board of Immigration Appeals, March 1, 1985.

76   *Ibid.*

77   *Ibid.*

78   *Ibid.*

79   19 I&N Dec. 211, 232 (BIA 1985).

interpretation of a social group was further complicated by another US interpretation known as the Social Visibility test. The Social Visibility test places emphasis on the extent to which members of a purported group would be recognizable to others in a society. While the Social Visibility test is a departure from precedent, it appears not to be an entirely new formulation as it bears a resemblance to Australia's Social Perception approach. However, the difference between Social Perception and Social Visibility is that Social Perception does not require the common attribute to be visible to the naked eye or the characteristic to be easily recognized by the general public, whereas Social Visibility does.

re CA

The importance of the Social Visibility test was first considered in *re CA*.[80] The issue to be addressed in *re CA*[81] was whether noncriminal informants constituted a particular social group for asylum purposes. In order to address the issue, the US BIA began with the interpretation of a particular social group in *Matter of Acosta*.[82] While affirming *Matter of Acosta's*[83] interpretation of a particular social group, the BIA discredited the Australian social perception approach by stating that: "we do not require a 'voluntary associational relationship' among group members. Nor do we require an element of 'cohesiveness' or homogeneity among group members."[84]

The BIA found that "noncriminal informants" did not constitute a particular social group because the group was too loose to meet the "particularity" requirement. However, as the respondent in his initial appeal referred to a subgroup of "former noncriminal government informants working against the Cali drug cartel," the BIA now considered whether former noncriminal government informants working against the Cali drug cartel constituted a different situation. This was because the cartel was now cohesive, despite the BIA's initial statement that cohesion did not matter.

Past Experience as an "Immutable Characteristic"

To reach a decision in *re CA*,[85] the BIA (applying *Matter of Acosta*) first considered whether the respondent's having informed on the Cali cartel was an immutable characteristic. While the BIA affirmed that a past experience is immutable on the basis that the event has already occurred and cannot be undone,[86] it does not

---

80   [2006] 23 I. & N. Dec. 951.

81   [2006] 23 I. & N. Dec. 951.

82   19 I&N Dec. 211, 232 (BIA 1985).

83   19 I&N Dec. 211, 232 (BIA 1985).

84   [2006] 23 I. & N. Dec. 951.

85   [2006] 23 I. & N. Dec. 951.

86   See also Matter of Fuentes [1988] 19 I&N 658, 662.

mean any past experience would constitute membership of a particular social group, and a guarantee of seeking asylum.[87] The BIA gave an example of a case[88] of those whose past experiences are immutable but are ineligible for asylum.

> For example, we do not afford protection based on social group membership to persons exposed to risks normally associated with employment in occupations such as the police or the military.[89]

The reason for this according to the BIA is that "... a person who agrees to work as a government informant in return for compensation takes a calculated risk and is not in a position to claim refugee status should such risks materialize."[90]

The BIA distinguished the respondent's actions in *re CA*,[91] from those employed by the government such as police officers. As the respondent emphasized that he did not inform on the Cali cartel for money, but out of moral responsibility and civic duty, the BIA focused on the question of whether the respondent's motives distinguished him from employed government officials such as the police. However, the

BIA held that the respondent did not constitute a particular social group because:

> Some persons employed as informants or otherwise receiving compensation as informants, including police officers, also act partly out of a sense of civic responsibility. Many such informants could plausibly claim that that their primary motivation was a sense of a civic duty and the compensation alone would not have provided sufficient incentive to undertake the risks involved. Therefore, the distinction between informants who are compensated and those who act out of civic motives is not particularly helpful ...[92]

Having found that the respondent did not qualify for membership of a particular social group under the criterion of *Matter of Acosta*,[93] the BIA turned to the issue of visibility.

The BIA adoption of the Social visibility criterion in *re CA*[94] seems to indicate that the fact that a characteristic is immutable or fundamental to identity is not enough to constitute membership of a particular social

---

87   [2006] 23 I&N Dec. at 958.

88   Matter of Fuentes [1988] 19 I&N 658.

89   [2006] 23 I. & N. Dec. 958.

90   Ibid.

91   [2006] 23 I. & N. Dec. 951.

92   [2006] 23 I&N Dec. at 959.

93   19 I&N Dec. 211, 232 (BIA 1985).

94   [2006] 23 I. & N. Dec. 951.

group. Under *re CA*,[95] a particular social group must also have social visibility.[96] In other words, like Australia's Social Perception, the group must be distinct and recognizable in a society to establish a particular Social Group. The BIA gave the example of members of the Marehan subclan of Somalia who could be said to constitute a particular social group.[97] According to the BIA, when it reached a decision that the Marehan subclan of Somalia were a particular social group, it: "... found that various clans could be differentiated based on linguistic commonalities as well as kinship ties."[98]

The BIA judgment in *re CA*[99] indicated that sharing the same characteristic was not enough to establish a particular social group, but also, that the characteristic must be socially recognized as distinct from the rest of the society.

In applying the social visibility test and denying the respondent claim for asylum, the BIA stated that:

When considering the visibility of groups of confidential informants, the very nature of the conduct at issue is such that it is generally out of the public view.

In the normal course of events, an informant against the Cali cartel intends to remain unknown and undiscovered. Recognizability or visibility is limited to those informants who are discovered because they appear as witnesses or otherwise come to the attention of the cartel members.[100]

Providing reasons for the introduction of social visibility as an additional requirement for the interpretation of a particular social group, the BIA cited the UNHCR *Guidelines*[101] as the main reason for the adoption of the Social visibility test when it stated that: "the recent Guidelines issued by the United Nations confirm that 'visibility' is an important element in identifying the existence of a particular social group."[102]

However, the BIA assertion is incorrect; a closer reading of the UNHCR *Guidelines* indicates that the UNCHR only articulated two approaches (*ejusdem generis* and Social Perception) in interpreting membership of a particular social group. It did not include or place emphasis on social visibility, which is probably a misinterpretation of the UNHCR *Guidelines* by the BIA.

---

95   [2006] 23 I. & N. Dec. 951.

96   [2006] 23 I. & N. Dec. 959.

97   [2006] 23 I. & N. Dec. 959.

98   [2006] 23 I. & N. Dec. 959.

99   [2006] 23 I. & N. Dec. 951.

100 [2006] 23 I. & N. Dec. 960.

101 2002 Guidelines on International Protection: Gender-Related Persecution within the context of Article 1A(2) of the 1951 Convention and/or its 1967 Protocol Relating to the Status of Refugees.

102 [2006] 23 I. & N. Dec. 960.

Even the UNHCR asserts that the BIA misapprehended its *Guidelines* in *Matter of Thomas*.[103] In its amicus brief in *Thomas*, the UNHCR stated that:

> It is not clear to us that the Board meant to adopt such requirement, particularly given that the Board in *Matter of C-A-* referenced the definition set forth in the UNHCR Guidelines on Membership of a Particular Social Group, which does not include a requirement that a particular social group meet the "social perception" test nor that the group be "socially visible."[104]

Additionally, the UNHCR maintains that:

> In sum, the combination of the "protected characteristics" and "social perception approach" in the UNHCR Guidelines on Membership of a Particular Social Group definition was intended to create alternative approaches for particular social group analysis rather than a dual requirement, and "social visibility" is not a requirement of the definition.[105]

The UNHCR statement above indicates that despite stating that *ejusdem generis* and Social Perception can be used in interpreting membership of a particular social group, it never intended for both approaches to be considered together in determining refugee claims. Rather, its intention was that courts begin with the *ejusdem generis* approach. Only if *ejusdem generis* fails can courts then consider using the social perception approach. Additionally, the UNHCR amicus clearly states that social visibility is not a requirement for the interpretation of membership of a particular social group.

Bresnahan also identified that the BIA misinterpreted the UNHCR *Guidelines*. Giving credit to the BIA for correctly highlighting "visibility" in the UNHCR *Guidelines*, Bresnahan maintains that the "Guidelines do not, as the BIA claims, establish social perception or social visibility as a requirement that must be met in order to determine membership of a particular social group."[106] To clarify what the UNCHR meant with the reference to "visibility" in its *Guidelines*, Bresnahan asserts that visibility was "meant to illustrate how being targeted can, under some circumstances, lead to the identification or even the creation of a social group by its members having been set apart in some way that has rendered them subject to persecution."[107]

---

103 *See* UN High Commissioner for Refugees (UNHCR), In the Matter of Michelle Thomas et al. (in Removal Proceedings). Brief of the Office of the United Nations High Commissioner for Refugees as Amicus Curiae, January 25, 2007, A-75-597-033/-034/-035/-036, http://www.refworld.org/docid/45c34c244.html (accessed October 16, 2013).

104 Ibid, 6.

105 Ibid., 9.

106 Kristin Bresnahan, "The Board of Immigration Appeals's New "Social Visibility" Test for Determining "Membership of a Particular Social Group" in Asylum Claims and Its Legal and Policy Implications," *Berkeley Journal of International Law* 29 (2011): 667.

107 Ibid., 667.

Furthermore, in *re CA*,[108] the BIA seems to have fallen into error on two counts. First, it deviated from the precedent established by *Matter of Acosta*[109] in interpreting membership of a particular social group. Second and lastly, it utilized the social visibility as a requirement while misinterpreting the UNHCR *Guidelines.* Several months later after deciding *re CA*,[110] the BIA also adopted Social visibility and treated it as a very important criterion in establishing a particular social group, in the case of *re AME*.[111]

re AME

In *re AME*,[112] the BIA considered whether "affluent Guatemalans" constituted a particular social group for refugee purposes. In making a decision, the BIA began with guideline interpretations of a particular social group set forth in *Matter of Acosta*.[113] Adopting Matter of Acosta's[114] first interpretation of a particular social group, the BIA reached a conclusion that, "wealth is not an immutable characteristic," and that the respondents were therefore not

members of a particular social group under *Matter of Acosta*.[115] However, the BIA did not exhaust the *Matter of Acosta*[116] guidelines by considering whether wealth was fundamental to identity; rather it hurriedly moved on to the issue of social visibility.

The BIA reaffirmed the importance of social visibility as a factor in determining a particular social group by citing *re CA*.[117] After citing passages from a country profile report on Guatemala which was at least a decade old, the BIA found that wealthy Guatemalans were not socially visible because, according to the 1997 Guatemala country profile and a Department of State 2001 country report, violence and crime were not only targeted at wealthy Guatemalans, but were "pervasive at all social-economic levels."[118]

While the BIA reached a decision that wealthy Guatemalans did not constitute a particular social group both under *Matter of Acosta*[119] and Social Visibility, it then went further to consider the issue of particularity in deciding whether affluent Guatemalans constituted a particular social group. In

---

108 [2006] 23 I. & N. Dec. 951.

109 19 I&N Dec. 211, 232 (BIA 1985).

110 [2006] 23 I. & N. Dec. 951.

111 [2007] 44 I&N. Jan. 69.

112 [2007] 44 I&N. Jan. 69.

113 19 I&N Dec. 211, 232 (BIA 1985).

114 19 I&N Dec. 211, 232 (BIA 1985).

115 [2007] 44 I&N. Jan. 73.

116 19 I&N Dec. 211, 232 (BIA 1985).

117 [2007] 44 I&N. Jan. 73.

118 [2007] 44 I&N. Jan. 74.

119 19 I&N Dec. 211, 232 (BIA 1985).

deciding the particularity of wealthy affluent Guatemalans, the BIA stated that, "wealth" and "affluent" were too amorphous to provide a benchmark for determining membership of a particular social group. Therefore, wealthy affluent Guatemalans could not be defined in a sufficiently distinct manner so that they would be recognized in Guatemala as a discrete class of persons.

The BIA also adopted the test of particularity and Social Visibility in determining whether a group of Salvadorian youths who have been recruited and have resisted gang membership, based on their own personal, moral, and religious values, were members of a particular social group.[120] In *Matter of S-E-G*,[121] the BIA did not apply *Matter of Acosta*[122] but rather immediately considered whether the groups of Salvadorian youths were sufficiently particular, and visible. Denying the respondents asylum, the BIA held that Salvadorian youths who resisted gang recruitment did not constitute a particular social group because they are not perceived as such by others in society, and as such cannot be recognized in El Salvador as a discrete class of persons.

A difference between the cases of *Matter of S-E-G*,[123] *re CA*,[124] and *re AME*[125] is that in *Matter of S-E-G*,[126] the BIA started by emphasizing that a group had to be particular in order to be seen as a particular social group. According to the BIA:

> The essence of the "particularity" requirement is whether the proposed group can accurately be described in a manner sufficiently distinct that the group would be recognized, in the society in question, as a discrete class of persons. While the size of the proposed group may be an important factor in determining whether the group can be so recognized, the key question is whether the proposed description is sufficiently "particular," or is too amorphous ... to create a benchmark for determining group membership."[127]

Applying the particularity standard, the BIA held that the respondents in *Matter of S-E-G*[128] lack particularity on the basis that they "make up a potentially large and diffuse segment of the society, and gang motivation in the recruitment and target of young males may arise from different perceptions."[129]

---

120 Matter of S-E-G- [2008] 24 I&N Dec. 579.

121 Matter of S-E-G- [2008] 24 I&N Dec. 579.

122 19 I&N Dec. 211, 232 (BIA 1985).

123 Matter of S-E-G- [2008] 24 I&N Dec. 579.

124 [2007] 44 I&N. Jan. 73.

125 [2007] 44 I&N. Jan. 69.

126 Matter of S-E-G- [2008] 24 I&N Dec. 579.

127 Ibid., 584.

128 Matter of S-E-G- [2008] 24 I&N Dec. 579.

129 Ibid., 585.

As the BIA held that the respondents were not particular enough, it went on to consider whether the group was socially visible. Denying the respondent's claim based on social visibility, the BIA stated that:

> There is little in the background evidence of record to indicate that Salvadoran youth who are recruited by gangs but refuse to join (or their family members) would be "perceived as a group" by society, or that these individuals suffer from a higher incidence of crime than the rest of the population.[130]

The two characteristics teased out of *Matter of S-E-G*,[131] namely "social visibility" and "particularity" in interpreting membership of a particular social group, have been met with mixed reactions from courts in the United States. For example, while the 1st,[132] 2nd,[133] 4th,[134] 8th,[135] 9th,[136] and 11th[137] Circuits have adopted Social Visibility and particularity in interpreting membership of a particular social group, it has been rejected by the 7th Circuit court in the United States.

Opposition Against Social Visibility

In *Gatimi v Holder*,[138] the 7th Circuit held that the BIA erred in applying the social visibility test, while denying the petitioner, Gatimi, asylum on the basis that there was no evidence that he possessed any "characteristics that would cause others in Kenyan society to recognize him as a former member of Mungiki."[139] Gatimi, a native of Kenya, was a member of Mungiki, a violent group, which "compels women, including wives of members and of defectors, to undergo clitoridectomy and excision."[140] A couple of years after joining the Mungiki, Gatimi defected, and there his problems began. As a result of his defection from the group, members of the Mungiki searched for him at his house. When they could not find him, they killed his servant. When Gatimi reported the incident to the police, they refused to help or protect him. A month after the first search, the Mungiki returned, looking for Gatimi's wife in order to circumcise her. However, they could not find her. As a result of this, Gatimi's wife fled to the United

---

130 Ibid., 587.

131 Matter of S-E-G- [2008] 24 I&N Dec. 579.

132 Scatambuli v Holder [2009] 558 F.3d 53.

133 Koudriachova v Gonzales [2007] 490 F.3d 255.

134 Lizama v Holder [2011] 629 F.3d 440.

135 Davila-Mejia v Mukasey [2008] F.3d 624.

136 Perdomo v Holder [2010] 611 F.3d 662.

137 Castillo-Arias v U.S Attorney General [2006] 446 F.3d 1190.

138 [2009] 578 F. 3d 611.

139 [2009] 578 F. 3d 617.

140 [2009] 578 F. 3d 613.

States with her newborn child.[141] On a third visit to Gatimi's home, the Mungiki killed Gatimi's family pets, burned two vehicles, and threatened to gouge Gatimi's eyes out. When he complained to the police, they promised protection, and on the basis of this promise, his wife returned back to Kenya. A week after her return, Gatimi was given an ultimatum by the Mungiki to produce his wife for circumcision within 2 weeks or he would be killed. Gatimi's wife went into hiding and subsequently returned to the United States, "followed shortly by Gatimi."[142]

Gatimi returned to Kenya couple of months later, having heard things had improved. He was kidnapped and tortured by the Mungiki, and was only released after he promised to produce his wife for circumcision. He finally left Kenya, and joined his wife in the United States, where he subsequently applied for asylum.

While the BIA reached a judgement that Gatimi et al. were not members of a particular social group, because they were not recognizable/visible in Kenyan society, the decision was met with heavy criticism by Judge Posner. According to Posner: "the only way, in the Board's view, that the Mungiki defectors can qualify as members of a particular social group is by pinning a target to their backs with the legend 'I am a Mungiki defector.'"[143]

Judge Posner maintained that the Board's reliance on social visibility in denying Gatimi et al. asylum was not only an inconsistent interpretation of a particular social group, the test "makes no sense,"[144] "nor has the Board attempted ... to explain the criterion of social visibility." In order to show that the Social visibility measure is a senseless interpretation of a particular social group, Judge Posner provides an example of "women who have not yet undergone female genital mutilation in tribes that practice it."[145] Such women, Judge Posner claims, would not be able to claim asylum under the Social visibility test, as their characteristic cannot be said to constitute membership of a particular social group.

Similarly, in *Benitez Ramos v. Holder*[146] the Social visibility test was also criticized by Judge Posner. Rejecting the Social visibility interpretation of membership of a particular social group in *Benitez Ramos v. Holder*,[147] the 7th Circuit held that an alien, who was a former member of Mara Salvatrucha (violent street gang), was a member of a particular social group within the meaning of the statute providing that persecution on the basis of membership in a particular social group was grounds

141 [2009]578 F. 3d 614.

142 [2009]578 F. 3d 614.

143 [2009]578 F. 3d 619.

144 [2009]578 F. 3d 617.

145 [2009]578 F. 3d 617.

146 [2009] 589 F.3d 426.

147 [2009] 589 F.3d 426.

for withholding of removal. Judge Posner described the Social visibility doctrine, which was rejected in *Gatimi v Holder*,[148] and now in *Benitez Ramos v. Holder*,[149] as a "misunderstanding of the use of 'external' criteria to identify a social group."[150] Judge Posner further gave an illustration of how visibility might be relevant to persecution, but maintained that Social Visibility was irrelevant to establishing a particular social group. According to Judge Posner:

> If society recognizes a set of people having certain common characteristics as a group, this is an indication that being in the set might expose one to special treatment, whether friendly or unfriendly. In our society, for example, redheads are not a group, but veterans are, even though a redhead can be spotted at a glance and a veteran can't be. "Visibility" in the literal sense in which the Board has sometimes used the term might be relevant to the likelihood of persecution, but it is irrelevant to whether if there is persecution it will be on the ground of group membership.[151]

Additionally, citing the case of *re A-M-E & J-G-U*,[152] Judge Posner maintained that the BIA appears to be confused when applying the social visibility test. To buttress his assertion, Posner observed that: "often it is unclear whether the Board is using the term 'social visibility' in the literal sense or in the 'external criterion' sense, or even whether it understands the difference."[153]

In addition to Judge Posner's criticisms of the social visibility doctrine which seems to have generated significant confusion and litigation, several academics have also challenged the social visibility and particularity as unreasoned departures from *Matter of Acosta*.[154]

Academic Debates on Social Visibility

Several scholars have discredited the Social Visibility test; this includes Pimentel, who maintains that social visibility test has led to a divide between US courts,[155] and Bresnahan, who argues that the sudden unexplained introduction of the social visibility test has made the "meaning of membership of a particular social group

---

148 [2009]578 F. 3d 611.

149 [2009] 589 F.3d 426.

150 [2009] 589 F.3d 432.

151 Ibid., 432.

152 [2007] 24 I.&N. Dec. 69.

153 [2009] 589 F.3d 430.

154 19 I&N Dec. 211, 232 (BIA 1985).

155 Melissa Pimentel, "The Invisible Refugee: Examining the Board of Immigration Appeals' "Social Visibility Doctrine," *Missouri Law Review* 76 (2011): 597.

more acute than ever."[156] Pimentel who describes social visibility as the "most controversial interpretation of the term particular social group"[157] asserts that the social visibility test would only lead to a great divide until there is an intervention by the US Supreme Court, or the BIA clarifies the social visibility doctrine.[158] Pimentel makes a solid argument on the basis that the chaos of the social visibility test can only be resolved by either the US Supreme Court or the BIA. However, as the social visibility and particularity test has been made an essential component in determining a particular social group by the BIA, it appears that the disturbance and rift the social visibility test has created among US courts can only be resolved by the US Supreme Court.

Bresnahan describes the Social Visibility test as not only a deviation from precedent as established by *Matter of Acosta*,[159] but also an inconsistent application of the law. To buttress her assertion, Bresnahan maintains that the BIA "has found groups to be par-ticular social groups without reference to social visibility." Bresnahan makes a correct assertion that can be supported with the BIA's judgment in *re CA*.[160] In that case, the BIA made reference to cases such as *re Kasinga*[161] and *Matter of Toboso-Alfonso*,[162] as possessing social visibility, whereas these were cases determined based on guidelines in *Matter of Acosta*.[163] According to Bresnahan, such cases which were determined with guidelines in *Matter of Acosta*[164] were cited by the BIA in order to artificially piece together a "visibility" requirement.

The Social Visibility test has been described as a difficult doctrine to apply. According to Marouf, the difficulty with applying the social visibility doctrine stems from the fact that the Social Visibility test is most subjective and sociological in nature, and it is not based on legal norms and principles like the "protected characteristic" approach; it poses unique evidentiary challenges and likely will result in inconsistent and incoherent decisions.[165]

---

156 Kristin Bresnahan, "The Board of Immigration Appeals's New "Social Visibility" Test for Determining "Membership of a Particular Social Group" in Asylum Claims and Its Legal and Policy Implications," *Berkeley Journal of International Law* 29 (2011): 651.

157 Melissa Pimentel, "The Invisible Refugee: Examining the Board of Immigration Appeals' "Social Visibility Doctrine," *Missouri Law Review* 76 (2011): 576.

158 Ibid., 597.

159 19 I&N Dec. 211, 232 (BIA 1985).

160 [2006] 23 I. & N. Dec. 951.

161 [1996] 21 I. & N. Dec. 357.

162 [1990] 20 I. & N. Dec. 819.

163 19 I&N Dec. 211, 232 (BIA 1985).

164 19 I&N Dec. 211, 232 (BIA 1985).

165 Fatma Marouf, "The Emerging Importance of "Social Visibility" in Defining a "Particular Social Group" and Its Potential Impact on Asylum Claims Related to Sexual Orientation and Gender," *Yale Law and Policy Review* 27 (2008): 71.

Furthermore, Bresnahan seems to provide the most concrete argument against the utilization of the social visibility test. According to Bresnahan, the Social Visibility test would exclude groups previously recognized as particularly social groups.[166] To support her argument, Bresnahan maintains that because of the invisibility of the traits at issue, asylum claims as regards to gender-related claims and those targeted by gang violence will be excluded based on the Social Visibility test.[167] Bresnahan makes a solid assertion. This is because, for example, victims of domestic violence may not meet the social visibility requirement, as domestic violence mostly occur in private settings. As a result of the danger posed by the Social Visibility test, Bresnahan calls for the revocation of the Social Visibility doctrine by the BIA.[168]

In agreement with Bresnahan, Marouf calls for the rejection of the Social Visibility test because not only does it destroy the principled framework of *Matter of Acosta*,[169] but it may also result in the denial of asylum claim by some of the most vulnerable individuals,[170] as also maintained by Bresnahan. Marouf provides a deeper analysis of the effect the Social Visibility test may have on asylum claims which are gender-related,[171] based on family membership,[172] and asylum claims relating to human trafficking.[173] Additionally, to further strengthen her argument as to why the Social Visibility test should be discarded, Marouf highlights the discretionary powers the Social Visibility test affords to decision makers. According to Marouf: "since the test is not law-based and social perceptions are so fluid, adjudicators will be able to deny freely the existence of a particular social group ... based on the finding that the group is not socially visible."[174]

Marouf appears to make a sound argument on the basis that the Social Visibility test is unprincipled. And as Marouf asserts, the discretionary powers afforded to decision makers by the Social Visibility test is further strengthened, as a definition has not been afforded to social visibility by the BIA.[175] On the basis of the arguments provid-

---

166 Kristin Bresnahan, "The Board of Immigration Appeals's New "Social Visibility" Test for Determining "Membership of a Particular Social Group" in Asylum Claims and Its Legal and Policy Implications," *Berkeley Journal of International Law* 29 (2011): 671.

167 Ibid., 671.

168 Ibid., 676.

169 19 I&N Dec. 211, 232 (BIA 1985).

170 Fatma Marouf, "The Emerging Importance of "Social Visibility" in Defining a "Particular Social Group" and Its Potential Impact on Asylum Claims Related to Sexual Orientation and Gender," *Yale Law and Policy Review* 27 (2008): 51.

171 Ibid., 88.

172 Ibid., 91.

173 Ibid., 98.

174 Ibid., 106.

175 Ibid., 106.

ed, and calling for rejection of the Social Visibility test, Marouf maintains that: "embracing the BIA's [social visibility test] not only will lead to chaotic case law and abdication of the United States' obligations under the Convention, but also will cause the legal community to reject the refugee status determination as a serious, principled process."[176]

However, irrespective of the arguments provided by Bresnahan and Marouf as to the dangers posed by the social visibility test and why it should be discarded, Soucek argues that "social visibility" only needs to be understood, not discarded.[177] According to Soucek,

> By reducing knowledge to sight, those adjudicating and litigating asylum cases have failed to "see" what the visibility criterion can contribute to our definition of social groups. Properly interpreted, the visibility criterion serves as a test of objectivity (or at least intersubjectivity); it prevents applicants from concocting ad hoc social groups in their quest for asylum. What it does not do is demand that individuals be visually recognizable as group members in order for courts to recognize their asylum claims.[178]

Soucek maintains further that Social Visibility is a metaphor, and groups are socially visible when a society sees itself, that is, thinks of itself as divided into such groups. While Soucek provides helpful analysis for the retention of the social visibility test, what he overlooks is that the Social Visibility test is an unnecessary complication of membership of a particular social group. Additionally, the UNHCR has cautioned the BIA against the utilization of the social visibility doctrine in its amicus brief in *Thomas*. The reason behind the caution according to the amicus brief is that a rigid approach such as social visibility "may disregard groups that the Convention is designed to protect."[179] In agreement with the UNHCR assertion above, same-sex-oriented persons seeking asylum encompass one of the vulnerable groups that may be affected by the US Social Visibility doctrine.

Impact of Social Visibility and Particularity on Refugee Claims Based on Sexual Orientation

Although same-sex-oriented persons have been recognized as a particular social group in the United States, under the guidelines laid out in *Matter of Acosta*,[180] this devel-

---

176 Ibid., 106.

177 Brian Soucek, "Social Group Asylum Claims: A Second Look at the New Visibility Requirement," *Yale Law and Policy Review* 29 (2010–2011): 338.

178 Ibid., 339.

179 UN High Commissioner for Refugees (UNHCR), In the Matter of Michelle Thomas et al. (in Removal Proceedings). Brief of the Office of the United Nations High Commissioner for Refugees as Amicus Curiae, January 25, 2007, A-75-597-033/-034/-035/-036, http://www.refworld.org/docid/45c34c244.html (accessed October 16, 2013), 10.

180 19 I&N Dec. 211, 232 (BIA 1985).

opment, with respect to same-sex-oriented claims, may be hampered by the Social Visibility test. Applying the Social Visibility doctrine to same-sex-oriented refugee claims requires lesbians and gay men to show that, on the basis of their sexuality, they are a perceived group in a society. While the Social Visibility doctrine requires that the group be visible to the eyes, same-sex-oriented persons who indulge in what Yoshino describes as "passing"[181] may not be able to claim asylum, irrespective of having a well-founded fear of persecution. Passing is the phenomenon whereby a same-sex-oriented person retains their same-sexuality, but due to the stigma attached to same-sexuality, the same-sex identity is masked. In societies hostile toward same-sexuality, same-sex-oriented persons sometimes mask their true identity by engaging in the heterosexual lifestyle in order to avoid persecution. Therefore, "passing," which reinforces "invisibility," becomes a way for same-sex-oriented persons to seek solace against stigma and persecution. The Inter-Church Committee on Human Rights in Latin America (ICCHRLA), in its special report, documents how same-sex-oriented persons in Latin America indulge in passing when it states that:

> In Latin America, as elsewhere, the social stigma associated with [same-sexuality] forces the majority of lesbians and gay men to hide their sexual orientation. The higher one is in the rigid socio-economic stratification present in many Latin American societies, the more one has to lose if one's [same-sexuality] is revealed. While all [same-sex oriented persons] experience various degrees of repression, the level and extent of abuses depends largely on the person's degree of "visibility" as a [same-sex oriented person] and the socio-economic position of the individual.[182]

The ICCHRLA statement above, which applies to many same-sex-oriented persons around the globe, demonstrates that passing is primarily a way for many same-sex-oriented persons to avoid rejection and persecution in societies to which they belong. The visibility of same-sex-oriented persons in societies hostile toward same-sexuality carries negative consequences in a same-sex-oriented person's family, the general public, and the State. For instance, in relation to the family, Silverstein and Picano[183] maintain that:

> For many gay men, one of the greatest downsides of coming out is that it sometimes means having to give up their natal family. It's

---

181 *See* Kenji Yoshino, *Covering: The Hidden Assault on Our Civil Rights* (Random house, 2006). Special thanks to Professor James Hathaway for the recommendation of this book.

182 ICCHRLA Special Report, Violence Unveiled: Repression Against Lesbians and Gay Men in Latin America (1996), 9.

183 Charles Silverstein and Felice Picano, *The Joy of Gay Sex: Fully Revised and Expanded Third Edition* (New York: HarperCollins, 2003).

sad but true that, for many families, there is no tolerance for gay children. For every mother who embraces her gay son after he's come out, there's another who curses him and tells him never to call or come back home ... many families, whether for religious or other reasons, don't outright disown and ban their [same-sex oriented children]. Instead they try to change them, ignore their lifestyle, or insist that, when they are at home, they follow the family's anti-gay rules. It can be stressful, and needless to say, as [same-sex oriented persons] grow older, their natural desire to have more to do with their family becomes deeply frustrated ... no wonder [same-sex oriented persons] form their own "families" and that increasingly they come to live within those fabricated families more intensely and fully than they would ever had done with their natal family.[184]

Silverstein and Picano's remarkable observation above, only applies to a few same-sex-oriented persons who are ready to face the consequences of visibility. However, for many same-sex-oriented persons, the fear of losing their natal family drives them to engage in passing, in order for their true identity to remain invisible. This invisibility or rather the indulgence in passing, according to Marouf, forms a core part of the experience of oppression suffered by same-sex-oriented persons.[185] In addition, Polanco maintains that, for many same-sex-oriented persons in their homelands, the side effects of passing result in panic and mental disorientation.[186] Another side effect of passing by same-sex-oriented persons is the constant indulgence in a foreign personality which translates to a life of misery. Additionally, by requiring the social visibility test, the BIA fails to take into account the evasive cost of passing by an invisible group such as same-sex-oriented persons. According to Yoshino: "these costs included the epistemic harm of alienation, the onerous labor of passing, the moral burden of doing so, and the ontic harm of identity erasure."[187]

Alongside these statements, Justice Albie Sachs of the Constitutional Court of South Africa provides the most eloquent statement indicating the BIA's ignorance in adopting the Social visibility test. According to Justice Albie Sachs:

In the case of [same-sex oriented persons], history and experience

---

184 Ibid., 105.

185 Fatma Marouf, "The Emerging Importance of "Social Visibility" in Defining a "Particular Social Group" and Its Potential Impact on Asylum Claims Related to Sexual Orientation and Gender," *Yale Law and Policy Review* 27 (2008): 79.

186 Jacqueline Jimenez Polanco, "The Dominican LGBTIQ Movement and Asylum Claims in the US," in *Migrant Marginality: A Transnational Perspective*, eds. Philip Kretsedemas, Jorge Capetillo-Ponce, and Glenn Jacobs (New York: Routledge, 2013), 170.

187 Kenji Yoshino, "Assimilationist Bias in Equal Protection: The Visibility Presumption and the Case of Don't Ask, Don't Tell," *Yale Law Journal* 108 (1998): 537.

teach us that scarring comes not from poverty or powerlessness, but from invisibility. It is the tainting of desire, it is the attribution of perversity and shame to spontaneous bodily affection, it is the prohibition of the expression of love, it is the denial of full moral citizenship in society because you are what you are, that impinges on the dignity and self-worth of a group ... [same-sex oriented persons] constitute a distinct though invisible section of the community that has been treated not only with disrespect or condescension but with disapproval and revulsion ... their identifying characteristic combines all the anxieties produced by sexuality with all the alienating effects resulting from difference ...[188]

Justice Sach's above assertion demonstrates that the BIA's adoption of Social visibility is myopic and poorly considered. This is because, in requiring social visibility to establish a particular social group, the BIA neglected to acknowledge the fact that groups such as same-sex-oriented persons use invisibility as a survival strategy to avoid persecution.

While the Social visibility test may be deemed useful for asylum claims based on gender, it may freeze out groups such as same-sex-oriented persons. The reason for this is because the Social Visibility criterion requires societal recognition, and because same-sexuality is not a visible characteristic, same-sex-oriented persons who indulge in passing, and thus not socially recognizable in a given society, may not be able to obtain asylum. It is clear that same-sex-oriented persons in intolerant societies indulge in passing so as to remain invisible in order to avoid persecution. Hence, it is evident that same-sex-oriented persons who remain invisible would not meet the social visibility requirement. On the basis of this argument, and reiterating Judge Posner's statement in *Gatimi v Holder*,[189] the Social Visibility test "makes no sense,"[190] and should be discarded.

Furthermore, the BIA's requirement of Social Visibility in the interpretation of a particular social group is arguably tantamount to the discretion policies rejected by the Australian High Court and the UK Supreme Court in *HJ (Iran)* and *HT (Cameroon)*.[191] By requiring social visibility to establish a particular social group, the US BIA is inadvertently saying that same-sex-oriented persons who remain discreet are not eligible for asylum because they do not face persecution, disregarding the fact that the suppression of a fundamental identity such as same-sexuality is persecution in itself. On the

188 Nat'l Coal. For Gay and Lesbian Equal. V. Minister of Justice 1998 (1) SA 1 (CC) paras. 127-28 (S. Afr.).

189 [2009]578 F. 3d 617.

190 [2009]578 F. 3d 617.

191 [2010] UKSC 31.

basis that there is a similarity between Social Visibility and discretion policies, the Social Visibility ought to be rejected by all US courts for this particular reason. It would not grant asylum to same-sex-oriented persons who do not live their lives freely for fear of persecution on the basis of their sexual orientation.

PART V

Conclusion

Based on the effect the Social Visibility test would have on refugee claims based on sexual orientation, all US Courts should reject the BIA's Social Visibility doctrine and continue to adopt the *Matter of Acosta*[192] approach in deciding such refugee claims. This is because, first, the introduction of the Social Visibility test by the BIA was unnecessary and destroys the principled interpretation of membership in a particular social group, as provided by *Matter of Acosta*.[193] Unlike the interpretive guidelines in *Matter of Acosta*,[194] the Social Visibility test, which places emphasis on the visibility of the group, can easily be utilized as a denial tool in rejecting same-sex-oriented asylum claims. This is because, in most societies where same-sexuality is deemed a negative behavior, same-sex-oriented persons would remain invisible in or-

der to avoid persecution, and therefore may not meet the threshold of the social visibility test. Finally, the Social Visibility test is also reminiscent of the discretion reasoning which has been rejected by the UK Supreme Court in *HJ (Iran)* and *HT (Cameroon)*.[195] This is because, similar to the previous point, by enforcing visibility, the Social Visibility test inadvertently creates discretion of same-sex-oriented persons, which has been rejected as an asylum concept because it violates the human rights of same-sex-oriented persons.

---

192 19 I&N Dec. 211, 232 (BIA 1985).

193 19 I&N Dec. 211, 232 (BIA 1985).

194 19 I&N Dec. 211, 232 (BIA 1985).

195 *HJ (Iran) and HT (Cameroon) v. Secretary of State for the Home Department*, [2010] UKSC 31, United Kingdom: Supreme Court, July 7, 2010, http://www.refworld.org/docid/4c3456752.html (accessed January 7, 2016).

Sperm Exchange on the Black Market: Exploring Informal Sperm Donation Through Online Advertisements

Ingrid Holme

School of Nursing & Midwifery, Trinity College Dublin, Dublin, Ireland

ABSTRACT

States tightly regulate citizens' bodies, their actions, and biological material, including organs, blood, and gametes, and this political governance involves a complex set of relationships between the state and its citizens. While new technologies persistently redefine family relationships, regulation and legislation are used to hold these fixed and static. Within sperm donation, the recipients transform into parents to form families, while the donor's identity and sexuality are considered to be unaffected by the action of donating sperm or gaining the status of sperm donor. Despite official efforts to sanitize the process, the practice of sperm donation is characterized in some quarters by efforts to evade or outflank the official restrictions on it. This paper explores the circumvention of such control, through examining informal sperm donation occurring outside of state regulation.

Keywords: Sperm, Donation, Regulation, State Control, Biopolitics.

摘要

各国都对其公民的身体，行为和包括器官，血液以及配子在内的生物材料有严格规定。这一政治治理涉及国家和公民间存在的一套复杂关系。虽然新科技持续不断地重新定义家庭关系，但法规却用于保持家庭关系不受变化。在精子捐赠中，接受者转变为父母的角色形成家庭，而捐赠精子或获得精子捐赠者身份的这一举动却不会影响捐赠者的身份和性向。尽管官方为消除这一过程做出了努力，精子捐赠的实践在某方面来说具有努力逃避或绕开官方对其限制的特征。通过检验发生在国家法规之外的非正式精子捐赠，本文对规避法律控制的行为进行了探索。

关键词：精子；捐赠；法规；国家对身体的管控；生物政治

RESUMEN

Los estados regulan estrechamente los cuerpos, sus acciones, materia biológica como órganos, sangre y gametos, y su gobernanza política involucra una red compleja de relaciones entre el estado y sus ciudadanos. Mientras que las nuevas tecnologías redefinen persistentemente las relaciones de familia, la regulación y la legislación se utilizan para mantenerlas fijas y estáticas. Dentro de la donación de esperma, los receptores se transforman en padres para formar familias, mientras que la identidad y la sexualidad del donante no se consideran afectadas por la acción de donar esperma o ganar el estatus de donante de esperma. A pesar de los esfuerzos oficiales para higienizar el proceso, la práctica de la donación de esperma se caracteriza en algunos sectores por los esfuerzos para evadir o superar las restricciones oficiales sobre el mismo. Este trabajo explora la elusión de ese control, mediante el examen de la donación informal de esperma, que ocurre fuera de la regulación estatal.

***Palabras clave:** Esperma, Donación, Regulación, Control estatal de los cuerpos, Biopolítica.*

"You haven't given me a gift; you've given me an obligation."
—Big Bang Theory 2008

Introduction

Nation states tightly regulate citizens' bodies, their actions, and biological material, including organs, blood, and gametes (Rose and Novas 2005). While there is a well-established scholarly debate regarding the biopolitics of women's bodies in reproduction (Cerwonka and Loutfi 2011; O'Riordan and Haran 2009; Rapp 2011; Waldby and Cooper 2008), there has been little substantive commentary on the issue of men's bodies and their material. This is particularly evident in relation to human sperm, where the practice of sperm donation has been subject to high levels of regulation and control. This paper explores how men and women circumvent such control, through examining informal sperm donation in the United Kingdom occurring outside of state regulation. These users rebel against a view of sperm as a material that must be controlled and guarded against and, in many cases, seek a recoupling of sex and reproduction.

While new technologies persistently redefine family relationships, regulation and legislation are used to hold these fixed and static (Blyth, Langdridge, and Harris 2010), and this requires instituting a specific cultural context for biological material. To protect sperm from commercialization, early sperm clinics promoted altruism as the key motivation for donors (Ragone 1999), and conceptualized sperm as a nonsexual gift from men (Daniels and Lewis 1996; Tober 2002). This has resulted in defensive commodification with the donor, recipient, and offspring, ascribing multiple emotional meanings to the sperm (Raphael-Leff 2010). In the United States, it has been shown that while the gendered application of altruism frames egg donation in feminine terms as the ultimate "gift," men are encouraged to consider sperm donation as an easy "job" (Almeling 2006, 2011). Alternative terms have been suggested for men who profit from their sperm: reproductive service worker (Almeling 2007), semen vendor (Annas 1980), semen provider, or supplier (Daniels 2007). Further to this, the Human Fertilization and Embryonic Authority (HFEA[1]), which regulates sperm donation in the United Kingdom, recently replaced the reimbursement of actual expenditure with a fixed sum (£35 per visit including expenses). As sperm clinics typically require men to make two donations per week for 6 months, they stand to make a total of £1680 (HFEA 2012), suggesting that in the United Kingdom sperm donation is becoming a form of voluntary work, part of a gift-based reproductive economy.

The HFEA (2005) promotes the image of sperm donors as "family men in their 30s (rather) than the old stereotype of hard-up medical students," with clinics regulating the type of man they considered worthy of donating, typical excluding those with nonheterosexual and low socioeconomic backgrounds (Almeling 2007; Yee 2009). For example, the Leicester Fertility Centre excludes men who were adopted and gay men for "the welfare and psychological well-being of any future children" (2011). The image of the sperm donor promoted by the HFEA is not only inaccurate regarding the typical sperm donor's age (Horsey 2005) but also fails to consider the impact of being a sperm donor upon the man's sexuality and kinship networks (i.e., their identity of being family men). Steinber (1997) has argued that *in vitro* fertilization (IVF) clinics hold a strong notion of reproductive fitness, based on eugenic reasoning, which reproduces heterosexuality, as both an end in itself and as the organizing logic. Within this setting, the recipients transform into parents and families, while the donor's identity and sexuality are considered to be unaffected by the action of donating sperm or the status of a sperm donor. This is questionable considering that, being a donor, a person regulates his/her sexual life during the six months of active do-

---

1   In 2010, the HFEA appeared on a list of quasi-autonomous non-governmental organization to be disbanded by the government (Raper 2010). It is not yet clear what practical change this will have on the regulation and governance of human gametes.

nation, as he/she must abstain from sex for 48 hours prior to the twice-weekly donation, and after this, there is a high likelihood that at least one of their children will decide to make contact with the man (and *his* family) upon reaching adulthood.

Despite official efforts to sanitize the process, the practice of sperm donation is characterized in some quarters by efforts to evade or outflank the official restrictions on it. One example is "the world's first donorsexual" (Culliford 2012), Trent Arsenaul, a 36-year-old self-confessed virgin and father of 16 children conceived through unregulated sperm donation (Dumas 2012). Trent reportedly forgoes physical sexual contact due to the risk of sexual transmitted diseases and modifies his nutritional intake to maximize sperm production. His sexuality, defined by his sperm donation and not by his "orientation" to the sex/gender of another person, poses a postmodern change to sexuality, not captured by the idea of asexuality. This paper, which examines traces of such activities on the Internet dating sites, has two aims. First, the paper provides a brief overview of informal sperm donation advertised on the Internet. Second, by looking at a sample of online advertisements, this paper highlights the nature of unofficial discourses of sperm donation. Focusing on altruism, families, and sexuality, this paper aims to open up a debate regarding the circumvention of state regulation surrounding reproduction. If we are to examine the way in which sperm donation is socially structured and culturally institutionalized, we must exam-

ine those who we consider outside of such settings to gain a full picture.

Black-market Sperm

The preceding century has been marked by creeping regulation of bodily material from organs, blood, and gametes, which conversely creates an alternative context for exchanging these items. When the *British Medical Journal* published the first contemporary academic account of sperm donation in 1945 (Barton 1945), the practice of sperm donation was largely unregulated, resulting in the author's husband playing a significant role in the number of children born in their London clinic, with estimates as high as 600 of the 1,500 children (Smith 2012). By 1984, the Committee of Inquiry into Human Fertilisation and Embryology recommended forming a licencing body. In 1990, during the debate of the Human Fertilisation and Embryology Act, the media covered the case of a 40-year-old lesbian receiving treatment from the Pregnancy Advisory Service. Deborah Lynn Steinberg has argued that the framing of this case as "selfish and deviant desires" of the woman involved led to the subsequent Human Fertilisation and Embryology Bill restricting treatment to those with male partners (Steinberg 1997). Formed in 1991 as the world's first "government fertility watchdog" (Raper 2010), the HFEA regulated sperm as a "gift" from anonymous men, so the recipient's husband was unchallenged as the child's father (Tober 2002). As donor-conceived children reached adulthood, there were increasing calls for them to be able to access the identity of their sperm donor. The HFEA removed donor anonymity in 2005, enabling those conceived from sperm donated after this date to access identifiable information at the age of 16. In the same year, the Science and Technology Committee considered the role of the Internet in sperm donation, drawing upon Mannotincluded.com Ltd, set up in April 2002, which produced "Britain's first known DIY internet baby" a year later (Galloway 2003). Compared to "known donor insemination" and "sex with a stranger," the committee felt that regulated services did not provide significant advantages, and applying regulation to Internet services was unlikely to shift users away from these unregulated approaches (House of Commons Science and Technology Committee 2005). The media coverage of Mannotincluded.com[2] illustrates the strong reaction to providing sperm to lesbians and single women making "selfish lifestyle choices." The activity was seen to "undermine the core values of family life" (Ballinger 2003) and to deny the child the chance to know his/her father. By 2005, the media coverage pointed to the medical doctor as an additional (typically male) missing figure: "I think it's better to have a medical involvement–it's not just man not included, it's man and doctor not included (Professor Ian Craft of the London Fertility Centre quoted in BBC 2005). The Human Fertilisation and Embryology Act was updated in 2008 to recognize partners in a same-sex relationship as

legal parents of children conceived using donated sperm, eggs, or embryos, and replaced the requirement for a father figure, with the need for clinics to consider the welfare of the child (HFEA 2008; see McCandless and Sheldon 2010 for the discussion of changes). However, the official sperm donation structure retained the assumption that all parties view the *ideal* conception of children as occurring within a dedicated monogamous relationship, which upon the child's birth transforms into a binary parenthood unit to provide a socially suitable environment for raising a child, even when the conception occurs in a clinic room by single women.

Within the official clinic, the man donates in a specialized room and the samples are "washed" and filtered so that "only the highest-quality sperm is used for the procedure" and the "concentrated sperm is passed directly into the woman's womb through a thin tube called a catheter" (NHS 2012). In this way, it is the clinic's work, and artificial insemination (AI) as a technology, that results in the transcendence of semen to reproductive material; hence, the socially acceptable technical solution to singleness, infertility, or the same-sex relationships is AI. Similarly, companies on the black market seek to bring about a parallel transformation, through their AI protocol. Free-Sperm-Donations.com, created in 2003, claims to have been used by over 24,000 women to have babies (FSDW 2011). This site describes the first steps of AI as the man ejaculating on his own and leaving the

---

2   The companies' nickname of *Morals Not Included* (Bracchi 2003) was reinforced in 2008 when the company director pleaded guilty to a number of charges related to financial misconduct.

sperm in a container for the woman to inject into herself. The site recommends purchasing the DIY Baby™ Ultimate Self-Insemination Kit which includes DIY Baby™ self-insemination guide, donor agreement document, pregnancy wheel and ovulation calculator, plastic syringe, sperm collection cup, 10 ovulation tests, 5 pregnancy tests, and folic acid. This produces an informal AI protocol which mimics the clinical nature of sperm banks and denotes a desexualization of the delivery system—syringe instead of penis. In 2007, SpermDirect. co.uk (aka Fertility1) became a test case for the state regulation of "fresh" sperm. In 2005, the HFEA considered the sperm used by Mannotincluded.com Ltd as outside of their sphere of regulation, as it was "fresh," unfrozen, and not stored (House of Commons Science and Technology Committee 2005). In contrast, SpermDirect.co.uk organized the transportation of the sperm from the donor to the recipient, and the HFEA issued the company with a notice that a licence was required; however, the company directors continued to dispute, resulting in the case being referred to the police. Subsequently, they were charged with processing and distributing sperm, and, in 2010, found guilty of illegally procuring sperm (Blackburn-Starza 2010). It would seem that the UK regulation around sperm donation has imbued human sperm with the rather strange status of being a controlled substance, which around half the population can self-manufacture.

According to the UK media, the removal of sperm donor anonymity in 2005 created a shortage of donors and an increase in "black-market sperm" (MacIntyre 2009).[3] This environment consists of brokerage websites (which arrange the packaging and transport of the sperm), connection websites (similar to Internet dating sites with members' profiles), as well personal classified advisements. Some sites cater to specific groups, such as Pride Angel, "a UK limited company founded by professional scientists Erika and Karen and a member of the gay business association" (Pride Angel 2012), while others, such as co-parentmatch.com accommodate those seeking co-parenting roles. One recent study of sperm-donors-worldwide.com, which facilitates a range of parenting options, indicated that the men offered similar motivations and a high level of altruism as to those from official sperm donors (Riggs and Russell 2010). Of the UK profiles, 72% of authors stated their motivation as a "wish to help others" followed by a wish to procreate (UK 18%), empathy (UK 7%), and valuable genetics (UK 3%). While the motivations offered by men may be similar to the structure surrounding, screening and identity checking are different. Some sites required men to document their identity and health status; however, the use of AI, rather than natural insemination (NI), causes the worry by the HFEA spokesperson "(a) donors might get their mate to donate in their place"

---

3   Compared to pre-2005 levels, identifiable donors have been reported as coming forward in lower numbers; over a 4-year period, 151 enquiries led to 14 donors, resulting in a marketing cost of approximately £5,500 each. (Tomlinson et al. 2010).

(quoted in Jeffries 2006). By 2010, the media coverage was increasingly concerned with personal advertisements and the HFEA warned women, "you put yourself at risk that the sample you receive is neither safe nor screened and that the donor is not who they say they are" (*Times* 2010). *Times'* article, "Shadowy world of web's unregulated fertility sites" focused on the "predatory intent" of the men, quoting a senior lecturer in Andrology (male reproductive health), now chairperson of the British Fertility Society, "They're in it purely for money. It's blatant profiteering" (*Times* 2010). To provide evidence of this claim, the male journalist advertised on a connection website, under the name Lucy. While the men offered to donate using both NI and AI, the article concluded they are "opportunists rather than full-on predators" and that these men were "exploiting vulnerable women and risking users' health and finances" (*Times* 2010).

Method

This study focuses on general classified online sites which were available to UK web users and revealed 49 advertisements (22 on Gumtree, 5 on freeclassifieds.co.uk, 22 on UKclassifieds.co.uk). The search began in October 2009 concentrating on Gumtree, which was UK's largest online classified website in the United Kingdom and Ireland (Brook 2005) and included sections such as accommodation as well as friendship and dating. The data set was expanded in 2012, using the same keywords, and although no new classifieds were found on Gumtree, advertisements were found on Freeukclassifieds.co.uk and UKclassifieds.co.uk. The lack of classifieds on Gumtree was probably due to the removal of the personal section following the robbery and murder of Leah Questin by a man she met on the site (Tozer 2010).[4] Variations of the keyword "sperm" were used and adverts that connected to sperm donation/donation or the mention of sperm for reproduction were included, so that the discarded advertisements concerned a range of topics including alternative medicine to increase sperm counts, pornographic DVDs, books about sperm whales, medical text books, etc. In cases where mobile phone numbers and email addresses were included in the texts, these were used as a search term in Google to find any additional advertisements. There are embedded ethical dimensions with using advertisements, especially those within "gated" communities; however, these advertisements were posted on free sites and no login details were required to post or read them. As this material was publically accessible via Google, no ethical approval was deemed necessary for this project.

These advertisements pose a number of analytical problems, unlike other studies which have used homogenous newspaper classifieds (i.e., Hogben and Coupland 2000). These texts are unconstrained by the social pres-

---

4   However this single act must be placed in perspective of the 642 murders which took place during 2010/11 (Chaplin, Flatley, and Smith 2011).

sures of being sent to a newspaper editor or the official clinical institutional structure and represent a "freer" expression than the personal profiles of official sperm donors, which are written within the clinical setting, given to the clinical staff etc. Overall, the UK personals were more structured than those on Gumtree, and many describe their physical features (i.e., body type, eye/hair color) as well as owning a car/house. However, the data set ranges in length, from 11 to 98 words, from formal English to abbreviated text speak, and in popularity being read between 4 and 1,474 times. In three cases, similar phrasing suggested that the advertisements were given by the same person (one sperm clinic published twice and two authors published three advertisements each). Faced with this heterogeneity, a qualitative content analysis using a loose set of priori codes was used to interpret meaning from the text data based on a coding scheme derived from the advertisements (age, physical description, intentions, and family) (Hsieh and Shannon 2005). Initially, a number of advertisements were read to fully develop the framework and this was then applied to the complete data set. Particular attention was paid to the differences between the advertisements. This paper highlights exemplars of the outliers. Ultimately, these are advertising texts which seek to catch attention and prompt a response, and the self-representation of motivations is to a certain extent framed by what the author considers is expected by the reader.

Advertising Sperm

Black-market work is concentrated in deprived populations and localities (Button 1984), and offers a survival strategy for the poor and unemployed (Elkin and McLaren 1991), suggesting that black-market sperm could represent an opportunity for individuals (and organizations) to access reproductive resources when excluded from official markets. This is borne out in by the range of classifieds found: 4 persons from sperm banks seeking to recruit donors and users, 10 seeking sperm and 36 offering sperm, which generally followed expected gender representations, with men offering sperm and women seeking sperm; however, there are a few examples of an infertile man and homosexual men seeking sperm. Of those advertisements that claimed a male gender, 18 mentioned their age (8 in their 20s, 3 in their 30s, and 7 over 40), suggesting that advertisers were younger and older than the ideal sperm donor sought by the official clinics. In addition, the advertisements frequently illustrate poor grammar and spelling (i.e., to/two, their/there, Sperm doner). In this way, the black market offers people outside of the desired age and education level of the official reproductive structure access to reproductive resources, and this, as this analysis shows, stimulates alternative formations of altruism, family, and sexuality.

A key difference between official and informal markets of sperm donation is the connection between the recipient and the donor, including the proprietorship and ownership of the biological material. Many of the advertisements from individuals illustrate this, for example,

> Hi any woman want my sperm so they can conceive?, NO strings, gay couple perhaps (*any woman want my sperm?* Gumtree 8)

This advertisement uses the possessive adjective "my" sperm to specify the relationship between the author and the biological material. Others use subjective pronouns to give prominence to the author's role, i.e., "I can help" (*want to get pregnant*, Gumtree 11 emphasis added) or a combination of possessive adjectives and subjective propounds, i.e. "**i** am **your** man" (*Sperm Donor Available For Lesbians Who Want A Baby,* Gumtree 6 emphasis added) and "a baby of **my own**, and **i** need someone to donate some of **their sperm**" (*could you help me out* Gumtree 9 emphasis added). This suggests that the lack of official structure enforcing separation of sperm/donor, donor/recipient, and donor/child enables authors to create, or at least suggests, atypical social interactions using the concept of sperm donation. The next three sections explore how the advertisements conceptualize this in terms of altruism, families, and sexuality.

Altruism and Benevolence

While the "gift" metaphor of sperm donation is clearly visible in the advertisements by official clinics, i.e., "Gentlemen, could you give the gift of life to childless couples?" (*Donors Urgently Needed Generous Expenses Paid* Gumtree 1), the majority of personal advertisement adverts use "helping" and "selling" as their frameworks. Gifting is about the giver, with what is given as symbolic of the nature of the relationship produced (Mauss 2002). Appeals to, and offers of, altruism are made by official clinics, women seeking sperm, and men offering sperm, with references to "help" appearing more frequently in advertisements from sperm clinics (3 out of the 4) and those seeking sperm donations (6 out of the 10) than men offering sperm (4 out of 35). The classifieds frequently illustrated the complex relationship between altruism and benefits to the donor. Three advertisements mention selling as men entering into a commercial arrangement, for example, one entitled *selling sperm*, notes "i like to sell my sperm to couples who wanted a baby and cant have any as there partners sperm count low (7 UKclassifieds.co.uk *selling sperm*). Similarly, in "*Sperm service available!*" Daniel illustrates the market nature of the activity, "i would like two sell my sperm two help people who carnt have kids for whatever reson it may be (...) am ere 2 help people and make people a family." (UKclassifieds.co.uk 16). His desire to help and make people into a (complete) family acts to also exclude him from this family, both in terms of emotional contact and financial obligation. In Daniel's case, the financial activity of selling his product, expressed within a context of altruism, illustrates the tension between men gaining payment for sperm, which in turn may result in children for which the state holds him financially accountable. Rather than "pure" altruism, benevolence, where both the donor and the recipient benefit including "feelings of warm glow," is increasingly recognized as a key motivation in blood donation (Ferguson, Farrell, and Lawrence 2008; Ferguson et al. 2012). Similarly, appeals to benevolence are found in advertisements from clinics, "All donors say how rewarding it feels to help couples to start families—something that most of us take for granted (*Donors Urgently Needed Generous Expenses Paid*, Gumtree 1), and is echoed by women seeking sperm, "There is no comeback on the guy. Just knowing you helped a couple have a child is an awarding experience" (*looking for a genuine man to help us,* UKclassifieds.co.uk 17). In this black market, there seems to be no conflict between seeking to sell sperm and mentioning seeking to help as a motivation; indeed, the linkage between the two activities is likely to be a positive one, as it signifies that the man is signing away his (parental) rights to the sperm and hence a child, which is the expectation when sperm is exchanged in official sperm donation.

Families and Kinship

In the classifieds, "family" is both an idealized dream and a marker of reproductive success. Without children, families are incomplete, and sperm clinics and their helpful donors can rectify this, "with your help we can give many more families the hope of completing their family" (*Sperm Donors Urgently Needed* Gumtree 2). The advertisements from sperm banks also direct their product at men who wish to "fulfil their dream of parenthood" (*The Reason Why Sperm Donation is Still On Top of the Infertility* UKclassifieds.co.uk 5). The similar *dream* of a family is shared by a lesbian couple who posted three advertisements (*Looking For An AI Sperm Donor* in Freeukclassifieds.co.uk 2; *Looking For A Genuine And Willing Man* in Freeukclassifieds.co.uk 3; and *Seeking AI Sperm Donor* in Freeukclassifieds.co.uk 4). They initially described themselves as a married lesbian couple seeking to "Make a Family of Our Dreams," which in the final advertisement becomes the self-representation as a "Loving Lesbian Couple," who have "Been Together a While and Now Decided We Want a Family." The text indicates that these two women do not constitute a family without a child, and hence without male involvement (see McCandless and Sheldon 2010 for a discussion of the unequal impact of sperm donation on homosexual and heterosexual families). One of the surprising findings was that only one author seeking sperm for reproduction referred to the desire to be a mother (wanted AI donor UKclassifieds.co.uk 20). More frequent were appeal for babies and children, for example, "im here to ask a request, im looking to have a baby of my own, and i need someone to donate some of their sperm" (*could you help me out* Gumtree 9). This is similar to IVF clinics which appeal to women through photographs of babies (Almeling 2007); however, in this case, babies are used to draw in male readers as sperm donors.

Families are critical for those advertisements offering sperm, as they mark the men as suitable sperm donors, providing evidence of reproductive capacity, and illustrate a tie to another committed family unit. For example, one person writes, "Hi Im [name] 43 A Healthy Father Of 4 Very Bright Cute Healthy Kids 3 With My Ex Wife And 1 With A Gay Couple I Helped A Bit Back (*Sperm Donor For Childless Woman/couple* Freeukclassifieds.co.uk 5). Another man references his "lovely girlfriend" as a marketing tool alongside his children, "i am a 23 year old mechanical engineer with 2 beautiful children and a lovely girlfriend" (*sperm donator wanting to help couples* Gumtree 10). Unlike official sperm clinics where differences in payment are due to treatment types (i.e., washed verses unwashed, fresh verses frozen), payment on the black market is for the sperm of that particular man, with lovely girlfriends and bright children. Advertisers also use other social aspects to promote their sperm as a valuable product (i.e., "good quality sperm!" *Do you want to get pregnant* Gumtree 10) including their own accomplishments such as engineering degrees (*Struggling to conceive ladies?* UKclassifieds.co.uk 3).

Some offers of sperm are connected to a lack of family, as men attempt access to family life and parenthood through sperm donation:

Single male 42 single looking 4 a couple or single lady who like to have a baby (...) looking to give a lady a child ,or couple ,v,w-el endowed,or poss meet a lady

who lik to settle down and start a family my no [...],v,genuine guy. (*Sperm donor* Gumtree 10)

While sexual motivations are clear as the author refers to being "well endowed," the reader is given the impression of the author also desiring what a child represents in terms of the life stage ("settling down" and "starting a family"). Similarly, the author of *"any lady needs a sperm donor?"* (Gumtree 13) is a "very busy, clean living man" would "like to have a son or daughter to give me a meaning in my life." The outcome of the interaction is concrete in this advertisement, mentioning a son or a daughter, visualizing the baby as a gendered individual. In these cases, where the men are seeking the social status of being a father, but willing to offer sperm donation, our attention is drawn to the fluidity of what it means to be a father.

The classified advertisements refocus attention onto the sexual nature of fathering, and the act of *begetting* a child:

I am a 40 year old man with 4 children who I adore. However, I have always wanted to father a child that I will have NO involvement with. (*Do you want to get pregnant?* Gumtree 12)

This advertisement provides an interesting contrast in motivations, seeking a woman who "want(s) to get pregnant" as the author desires to "father a child." The author expresses the desire to achieve "fathering" without assuming the obligations and responsibility of being "a" father, and in doing so seeks to illustrate virileness, both in terms of biological capacity and social capacity to escape state labeling as a father. In this case, the author notes that "obviously, I cannot accommodate," suggesting that the mother of his children will not be informed of his informal sperm donation. The advertisement highlights conflicting ideas about *fathering* children, and the connection to sperm donation. On the one hand, the author portrays himself as a "good father" stating that he "adores" his four children, but on the other hand, he wants to "father" children he has no involvement with. This contrasts strongly with state regulation that holds the sperm donor legally and financial responsible for children produced outside of the sperm bank. Within the state framework, the author markets himself as a *good father* but offers his sperm within the context of being a *bad father*.

On the black market, family and children clearly represent success in terms of both reproduction and social status. The offer by some men to donate sperm in the same advertisement as seeking a woman to have their child raises questions as to how separate these activities are for men. Physiological differences between females and males create unequal capacities to have a child, to bear and beget a child. This has translated into differing health structures which enable a woman's desire to be a mother and bear a child to be fulfilled through state-sponsored sperm donation, the recipient of the "gift" of sperm, whereas, as a man, is re-

duced to the role of "donor" of a child through sperm donation.

Sexuality

Sex enters the advertisements in a range of ways, from suggestions of natural conception to the outright statement of sexual acts. Mention of pregnancy is prevalent in the advertisements, and range from those where sperm donation seems the main intent, for example, "want to get pregnant", which offers "Guaranteed results! (well almost) Good quality sperm!" (Gumtree 10) to those which suggested that penetrative sex is the main intention. One author states that the type of activity (penetrative sex without condom) is more important than the age and "look" of the woman reading the classified: "age and look are not important. What's important is that you want to get pregnant" (Gumtree 11). This suggestive language is also seen in one of the rare advertisements from a woman.

> Looking for a guy to get me pregnant, must have classic good looks, and a bit of brains. Must be able to accommodate. Best offer by 6 pm, and I can see you tonight. I'm 33, size 10, Blonde. (*make me pregnant* Gumtree 18)

This was by far the most popular advertisement found on Gumtree, opened 1,474 times. Here, the author seems unlikely to intend to pick the father of her future child by "best offer by 6 pm tonight"; instead, this, and the other advertisements are more likely directed at offers of "unprotected" sex. Others, such as "sperm donors wanted" where the author is "Looking for virile males who want to donate their sperm to a good cause" (Gumtree 19) connects this highly masculine identity, the male impregnator, to sperm donation. This post shows the connection with sperm donors and request for "virile" males to "donate their sperm to a good cause" which makes explicit references to fellatio rather than hand stimulation, similar to the advertisements directed at "making" the woman pregnant. In addition, advertisements from both heterosexual and homosexual authors expand on the virility of the official sperm donor by referring to a "sperm bank" opening and seeking deliveries/deposits and grateful acceptance of sperm. The advertisement entitled "Sperm Bank Opening" plays with the idea of a person performing the role of a sperm bank, where "collections now being made in your area" (Gumtree 20). The author of "Mature sperm bank wishes to make a deposit" seeks a woman for similar use (Gumtree 21). These two advertisements suggest that being a sperm donor ties to active masculinity performed by the male partner in a heterosexual context, while being the sperm bank is the passive, receptive role in homosexual fetishism and female in the heterosexual context.

Conclusion

The gift framework has conceptualized the exchange of biological material as driven by altruistic motivations, while paying little heed to the corresponding obligation of reciprocity embedded within the act of gifting. The state excludes people who seek to gain financially from their biological material; implying that these impure motivations would have led the person to engage in dangerous behavior which is likely to taint the biological material with sexual diseases, as illustrated by the HFEA's comments mentioned in the introduction regarding black-market sperm. What is also at stake is control over the biological material as a (financial) resource and the state regulation of parental obligations. Recognizing that a person may seek to sell their material and consider it as their own resource, which can function without the involvement of medical doctors or laboratory equipment, challenges the medical governance of reproduction. In the formal governed structure, the emphasis is upon knowing who, in social, psychological, and biological terms, the donor is, so that the medical staff may judge his worth as a sperm donor. Hence, the online classified advertisements, posted by near anonymous people, offer a challenge to the state's demanding need to be able to identify biological fathers, and hold them accountable, both socially and financially, for their children. This is illustrated the UK's Child Support Agency pursuit of informal sperm donors for financial support, although recently the legal position has changed for cases where the mother is in a civil partnership (Brignall 2012). Hierarchies of respectability and good citizenship exist among heterosexuals, with traditional gender arrangements and lifelong monogamy at the top (Seidman 2005). Further empirical research is needed to fully probe the concerns of regulators and sperm clinics as to the threat posed by informal sperm donation on the black market to these hierarchies.

Arguably, sperm embodies the extremes of masculinity, "the best and worst notions of what we think it is to be a man" (Moore 2007, 96), and the black market displays this range of extremes. As this paper has shown, families and kinship are important to the authors selling sperm who are already fathers in a nuclear family as well as those "barren" men who are offering sperm as a way of gaining parenthood. What this paper suggests is that these men offer sperm due to varying degrees of benevolence, and framing the exchange as "selling" cuts men's ties to the sperm (and who it may become), benefiting both themselves and the women who want a baby of *their own*. In terms of sexual identity, these advertisements are a small proportion of the over million online classifieds for a sexual partner (Aral and Manhart 2009); however, as these advertisements show, the image of the sperm donor enters into sexual activity. "Stranger sex" which, many of the advertisements suggest, runs contra to the nature of monogamous relationships, where dating and subsequent sexual activity are aimed at forming a fixed and static unit. NSA (no strings attached) fun, a euphemism for sexual activity outside of a committed relationship, has been the public health target for the last 30 years about protected sex (i.e., condom use) and sexually transmitted diseases. "Safe

sex" campaigns conceptualized heterosexual vaginal penetrative sex as risky, unsafe, and resulting in pregnancy, so that to "protect" against this, an active choice must be taken to use condoms. Regulation concerning sperm has focused on its reproductive nature; however, responsible adults are expected to follow the safe-sex messages of public health where sperm is captured in a container coated with spermicide, with protection against both its reproductive and disease potential. It is striking that many of these advertisements rebel against this view of sperm as a material that must be controlled and guarded against. It would seem that by taking part in the activity on the black market, men and a few women seem to have found a way to express emotional and mental desires about who they would like to become by imagining conceiving children both in terms of parents and as sexual beings. The image of the sperm donor offers a fantasy where masculine potency can play a leading role, tied to the act of *making* a woman pregnant, indicating the undercurrent attraction to the power of a man to impregnate. Further research is needed to explore, from the perspective of those involved, the meaning and actions in which they engage. If one accepts that academic debates with regard to sperm donation must also incorporate those who refer to the concept for activities traditionally understood as unproduced sex, one night stands and casual sex, then the future research agenda is wide ranging. There is clearly a need to trace the online activity and attempt to access the voices of the authors and readers of such posts, and explore the international context. In similarity with the attribution of female heterosexual liberation to the contraception pill, additional research may find that black-market sperm donation has separated fathering from being a father, but also enabled a reconnection between penetrative sex, sperm, and the primeval fantasy of pregnancy. In addition, empirical research is necessary to establish how official structures such as the officers of the Child Benefit Office act when faced with unofficial sperm donation.

References

Almeling, R. 2006. "Why Do You Want to Be a Donor?: Gender and the Production of Altruism in Egg and Sperm Donation." *New Genetics and Society* 25 (2) 143–157.

Almeling, R. 2007. "Selling Genes, Selling Gender: Egg Agencies, Sperm Banks, and the Medical Market in Genetic Material." *American Sociological Review* 72 (3): 319–340.

Almeling, R. 2011. *Sex Cells: The Medical Market for Eggs and Sperm*. Berkeley: University of California Press.

Annas, G. J. 1980. "Fathers Anonymous: Beyond the Best Interests of the Sperm Donor." *Family Law Quarterly* 14 (1): 1–13.

Aral, S. O., and L. E. Manhart. 2009. "Someone Naughty for Tonight: Sex Partner Recruitment Venues and Associated STI Risk." *Sexually Transmitted Infections* 85 (4): 239–240.

Ballinger, L. 2003. "Men not Included." *Wales on Sunday*. Accessed 17 August 2003. http://www.walesonline. co.uk/news/wales-news/content_ objectid=13302304_method=full_ siteid=50082_headline=-Men-not-included-name_page.html.

Barton, M. 1945. "Artificial Insemination." *British Medical Journal* 1 (277): 144.

BBC. 2005. "Web Sperm Sites Crackdown Planned." Accessed 21 November 2012. http://news.bbc.co.uk/1/hi/ health/4145378.stm.

Big Bang Theory. "*The Bath Item Gift*." Series 2 (2008) Episode 11. Chuck Lorre Productions.

Blackburn-Starza, A. 2010. "Men Convicted Over Illegal Sperm Website." *Bionews*. Accessed 21 November 2012. http://www.bionews.org.uk/ page_71051.asp.

Blyth, E., D. Langdridge, and R. Harris. 2010. "Family Building in Donor Conception: Parents' Experiences of Sharing Information." *Journal of Reproductive and Infant Psychology* 28 (2): 116–127.

Bracchi, P. 2003. "Morals Not Included." *Daily Mail*. Accessed 21 November 2014. http://www.highbeam.com/ doc/1G1-107099782.html.

Brignall, M. 2012. "Gay Sperm Donor

Told to Pay Child Maintenance for 'His' Two Children." *The Guardian*. Accessed 26 October 2012. http://www.guardian.co.uk/money/2012/oct/26/gay-sperm-donor-pay-child-support-maintenance.

Brook, S. 2005. "eBay Buys London Ads Website Gumtree." *The Guardian*. Accessed 21 November 2014. http://www.guardian.co.uk/media/2005/may/19/business.newmedia.

Button, K. 1984. "Regional Variations in the Irregular Economy: A Study of Possible Trends." *Regional Studies* 18 (5): 385–392.

Cerwonka, A., and A. Loutfi. 2011. "Biopolitics and the Female Reproductive Body as the New Subject of Law." *feminists@ law* 1 (1). Accessed 21 November 2014. http://journals.kent.ac.uk/index.php/feministsatlaw/article/view/18/77.

Chaplin, R., J. Flatley, and K. Smith. 2011. *Crime in England and Wales 2010/11 Findings from the British Crime Survey and Police Recorded Crime*. 2nd ed. Accessed 21 November 2014. http://www.homeoffice.gov.uk/publications/science-research-statistics/research-statistics/crime-research/hosb1011/hosb1011?view=Binary.

Culliford, G. 2012. "I've Fathered 16 Children But I'm Still a Virgin at 36." *The Sun*. Accessed 21 November 2014. http://www.thesun.co.uk/sol/homepage/features/4351383/Trent-Arsenault-I-have-fathered-16-children-but-I-am-still-a-virgin-aged-36.html.

Daniels, K. R. 2007. "Anonymity and Openness and the Recruitment of Gamete Donors. Part 1: Semen Donors." *Human Fertility* 10 (3): 151–158.

Daniels, K. R., and G. M. Lewis. 1996. "Donor Insemination: The Gifting and Selling of Semen." *Social Science and Medicine* 42 (11): 1521–1536.

Dumas, D. 2012. "'Organic' Sperm Donor Who has Fathered 14 Children Admits He is a 36-Year-Old VIRGIN." *Daily Mail*. Accessed 21 November 2014. http://www.dailymail.co.uk/femail/article-2087522/Virgin-father-14-kids-Sperm-donor-Trent-Arsenault-admits-hes-36-year-old-VIRGIN.html.

Elkin, T., and D. McLaren. 1991. *Reviving the City: Towards Sustainable Urban Development*. London: Friends of the Earth.

Ferguson, E., K. Farrell, and C. Lawrence. 2008. "Blood Donation is An Act of Benevolence Rather than Altruism." *Health Psychology* 27 (3): 327–336.

Ferguson, E., M. Taylor, D. Keatley, N. Flynn, and C. Lawrence. 2012. "Blood Donors' Helping Behavior is Driven by Warm Glow: More Evidence for the Blood Donor Benevolence Hypothesis." *Transfusion* 52 (10): 2189–2200.

Free Sperm Donations Worldwide. 2011. Accessed 21 November 2014. http://www.free-sperm-donations.com/.

Galloway, E. 2003. "Couples to Have First

DIY Internet Babies; PARTNERS PAY £830 TO WEBSITE FOR SPERM TO BE DELIVERED TO THEIR HOMES." *Evening Standard*, London. Accessed 21 November 2014. http://www.questia.com/library/1G1-104471058/couples-have-first-diy-internet-babies-partners-pay.

Hogben, S., and J. Coupland. 2000. "Egg Seeks Sperm: End of Story: Articulating Gay Parenting in Small Ads for Reproductive Partners." *Discourse and Society* 11 (4): 459–485.

Horsey, K. 2005. "The HFEA's Father Figures: Lies, Damn Lies and Statistics?" *BioNews*, 329, October 10. Accessed 21 November 2014. http://www.bionews.org.uk/page_37828.asp.

House of Commons Science and Technology Committee. 2005. *Human Reproductive Technologies and the Law: Fifth Report of Session 2004–2005*. Volume II: Oral and Written Evidence. HC-7-II, Ev 83–Ev 93. London: The Stationary Office. Accessed 21 November 2014. http://www.publications.parliament.uk/pa/cm200405/cmselect/cmsctech/7/7i.pdf.

Hsieh, H. F., and S. E. Shannon. 2005. "Three Approaches to Qualitative Content Analysis." *Qualitative Health Research* 15 (9): 1277–1288.

Human Fertilisation and Embryology Act. London: The Stationery Office, 2008. Accessed 21 November 2014. http://www.legislation.gov.uk/ukpga/2008/22/contents.

Human Fertilisation and Embryology Authority. 2005. "Who are the UK's Sperm Donors? Fertility Regulator Presents National Picture of the People Who Donate." Accessed 21 November 2014. http://www.hfea.gov.uk/669.html.

Human Fertilisation and Embryology Authority. 2006. "What You Need to Know About Using Donated Sperm, Eggs or Embryos in Your Treatment." Accessed 21 November 2014. http://www.hfea.gov.uk/docs/What_you_need_to_know_about_using_donated_sperm_eggs_or_embryos.pdf.

Human Fertilisation and Embryology Authority. 2006. "HFEA Agrees New Policies to Improve Sperm and Egg Donation Services." Accessed 21 November 2014. http://www.hfea.gov.uk/6700.html.

Human Fertilisation and Embryology Authority. 2012. "Sperm Donation." Accessed 26 December 2016. http://www.hfea.gov.uk/sperm-donation-eligibility.html.

Jeffries, S. 2006. "Who's the Daddy?." *The Guardian*, Saturday, November 18. Accessed 21 November 2014. http://www.guardian.co.uk/society/2006/nov/18/health.lifeandhealth.

Leicester Fertility Centre. 2001. *Information for Sperm Donors*. Accessed 21 November 2011. http://www.leicesterfertilitycentre.org.uk/userfiles/SpermDonorinformation.pdf.

MacIntyre, D. 2009. *5live Sunday*. Accessed 21 November 2014. http://www.bbc.co.uk/programmes/b00mtqw5

Mauss, M. 2002. *The Gift: The Form and Reason for Exchange in Archaic Societies*. Abingdon: Routledge.

McCandless, J., and S. Sheldon. 2010. "The Human Fertilisation and Embryology Act (2008) and the Tenacity of the Sexual Family Form." *The Modern Law Review* 73 (2): 175–207.

Moore, L. 2007. *Sperm Counts Overcome by Man's Most Precious Fluid*. New York: New York University Press.

NHS. *How Artificial Insemination is Performed—NHS Choices*. Accessed 21 November 2014. www.nhs.uk/conditions/Artificial-insemination.

O'Riordan, K., and J. Haran. 2009. "From Reproduction to Research Sourcing Eggs, IVF and Cloning in the UK." *Feminist Theory* 10 (2): 191–210.

Pride Angel. Accessed 21 November 2014. http://www.prideangel.com/p4/.

Ragone, H. 1999. "The Gift of Life: Surrogate Motherhood, Gamete Donation, and Constructions of Altruism." In *Transformative Motherhood: On Giving and Getting in a Consumer Culture*, edited by Linda L. Layne, 65–68. New York: New York University Press.

Raper, V. 2010. "New Breed of Fertility Watchdog on Way." *BioNews* 568. Accessed 21 November 2014. http://www.

bionews.org.uk/page_67397.asp.

Raphael-Leff, J. 2010. "The Gift of Gametes—Unconscious Motivation, Commodification and Problematics of Genealogy." *Feminist Review* 94 (1): 117–137.

Rapp, A. 2011. "Reproductive Entanglements: Body, State, and Culture in the Dys/Regulation of Child-Bearing." *Social Research: An International Quarterly- Social Research* 78 (3): 693–718.

Riggs, D. W., and L. Russell. 2010. "Characteristics of Men Willing to Act As Sperm Donors in the Context of Identity-Release Legislation." *Human Reproduction* 26 (1): 266–272. Accessed 21 November 2014. http://humrep.oxfordjournals.org/content/early/2010/11/17/humrep.deq314.full.pdf.

Rose, N., and C. Novas. 2005. "Biological Citizenship." In *Global Assemblages: Technology, Politics, and Ethics as Anthropological Problems*, edited by Aihwa Ong and Stephen J. Collier, 439–463. Oxford: Blackwell.

Seidman, S. 2005. "From the Polluted Homosexual to the Normal Gay: Changing Patterns of Sexual Regulation in America." In *Thinking Straight: The Power, Promise and Paradox of Heterosexuality*, 39–61. edited by C. Ingrahamh. New York: Routledge.

Smith, R. 2012. "British Man 'Fathered 600 Children' at Own Fertility Clinic." *Telegraph*, April 8. Accessed 21 November 2014. http://www.telegraph.co.uk/news/9193014/British-man-fathered-600-children-at-own-fertility-clinic.html.

Steinberg, L. D. 1997. *Bodies in Glass: Genetics, Eugenics, Embryo Ethics*. Manchester: Manchester University Press.

Times. 2010. "Shadowy World of Web's Unregulated Fertility Sites." *The Times*. Accessed 21 November 2014. http://www.gambleandghevaert.com/blog/2010/07/19/times-article-on-unregulated-fertility-sites-quotes-natalie-gamble/.

Tober, D. 2002. "Semen As Gift, Semen As Goods: Reproductive Workers and the Market in Altruism," In *Commodifying Bodies*, edited by N. Scheper-Hughes and L. Wacquant, 136–161. London: Sage.

Tomlinson, M. J., K. Pooley, A. Pierce, and J. F. Hopkisson. 2010. "Sperm Donor Recruitment Within an NHS Fertility Service Since the Removal of Anonymity." *Human Fertility* 13 (3): 159–167.

Tozer, J. 2010. "Conman Who Murdered Care Worker He Met Online then Dumped Her Body in a Suitcase Jailed for Life." *Daily Mail*. Accessed 21 November 2014. http://www.dailymail.co.uk/news/article-1291286/Conman-murdered-care-worker-met-online-dumped-body-suitcase-jailed-life.html.

Waldby, C., and M. Cooper. 2008. "The Biopolitics of Reproduction." *Australian Feminist Studies* 23 (55): 57–73.

Yee, S. 2009. "'Gift Without a Price Tag': Altruism in Anonymous Semen Donation." *Human Reproduction* 24 (1): 3–13.

A Study in LGBTQ Activism in Serbia and Russia after 1991: Different Countries, Common Issues?

Batueva Ekaterina
President at Youth Included, Prague, Czech Republic

Đorđević Vladimir

Assistant Professor at Faculty of Regional Development and International Studies, Mendel University, Brno, Czech Republic

ABSTRACT

This article is dedicated to examining the issue of LGBTQ activism in Serbia and Russia after 1991. Considering the fact that these countries were republics in two former socialist federal states, it is interesting to investigate the position of the LGBTQ community and conclude on the influence of this community in challenging the political and social status quo in both societies. Moreover, citizens of Serbia and Russia are understood to be predominantly Orthodox Christian, with generally pervasive patriarchal social attitudes, and this point makes a comparative perspective even more interesting. Hence, this article proposes to provide concise historical information on both communities in their respective states after 1991 when both the USSR and SFR Yugoslavia disappeared. Brief historical information will be presented only to introduce major developments in the existence of the said community and its position in both societies. Second, the article is aimed at discussing and comparing the major political and social constraints in both states on the LGBTQ community and its functioning. Lastly, the article seeks to present conclusions on whether the said community has so far had any influence in terms of being a possible "driver" of political and social changes, or it has remained but a mere object rather than subject in the social and political life.

Keywords: LGBTQ, Social activism, Serbia, Russia, Historical perspective, Comparative perspective, Social change

摘要

本文致力于检验1991年后塞尔维亚和俄罗斯地区LGBTQ行动主义的问题。考虑到这两个国家都曾是社会主义联邦共和国这一事实，不论是调查LGBTQ社区的地位，还是总结该社区在挑战各自政治和社会现状时所产生的影响，都将是相当有趣的体验。不仅如此，大部分塞尔维亚和俄罗斯公民都被认为是基督东正教徒，他们基本上都有着浓厚的父系社会态度——这一点使得两国的比较视角更加有趣。因此，本文首先为1991年苏联（简称USSR）和南斯拉夫社会主义联邦共和国（简称SFR Yugoslavia）分别解体后俄罗斯和塞尔维亚两国的LGBTQ社区提供了简明的历史信息（该简明信息仅用于介绍两社区所存在的重大发展以及其地位）。第二，本文讨论并对比了两国的主要政治限制和社会限制，用于总结LGBTQ社区扮演的角色和功能。最后，本文将所得的不同结论进行呈现，这些结论包括：1.目前社区是否可能"驱动"政治和社会变化，从而造成任何影响；2. 社区仅仅是社会和政治生活中的一个客体，而非主体。

关键词： LGBTQ，社会行动主义，塞尔维亚，俄罗斯，社会变化，社区发展，国家控制

Resumen

Este artículo examina la cuestión del activismo LGBTQ en Serbia y Rusia después de 1991. Tomando en consideración el hecho de estos países fueron repúblicas en dos antiguos estados federales socialistas, resulta interesante investigar la posición de la comunidad LGBTQ y llegar a alguna conclusión acerca de la influencia de dicha comunidad en el cuestionamiento del status quo político y social en ambas sociedades. Asimismo, los ciudadanos de Serbia y Rusia son considerados como cristianos ortodoxos, con actitudes sociales que son generalmente patriarcales e invasivas, y dicha consideración hace que esta perspectiva comparativa sea aún más interesante. Por consiguiente, este artículo se propone, primero que todo, proveer información histórica concisa en relación a ambas comunidades en sus respectivos estados y después de 1991, cuando tanto la Unión Soviética (URSS) como la República Federativa Socialista de Yugoslavia (RFS Yugoslavia) desparecieron. Esta información histórica será presentada con el objetivo de presentar los desarrollos más importantes de dicha comunidad y su posición en ambas sociedades.

En segundo lugar, en este artículo se discutirá y comparará los constreñimientos políticos y sociales más significativos en ambos estados para así determinar si dicha comunidad ha logrado tener alguna influencia en cuanto a ser promotora de cambios políticos y sociales, o si ha permanecido como un mero objeto más que sujeto en la vida social y política.

Palabras clave: LGBTQ, Activismo Social, Serbia, Rusia, Cambio Social, Desarrollo Comunitario, Control Estatal.

Introduction

This article is a case study covering LGBTQ activism in Serbia and Russia after 1991, and it is based on both data and analyses presented in official government reports on the issues at hand, as well as various national and international LGBTQ organizations' publications in this respect. In addition, the paper also takes into consideration reports published by numerous NGOs and international organizations which specialize in the field. In that respect, this essay, on the one hand, discusses LGBTQ activism in Serbia and Russia after 1991 by introducing a brief historical perspective on the LGBTQ community in both states. On the other hand, it also discusses major political and social constraints that, in both cases, have hindered the aforementioned community and its functioning. Lastly, the paper states the similarities and differences between Serbia and Russia based on the data discussed here.

It is worth noting that this comparative case study covers the period from 1991 to 2014 alone, and that it is based on the notion that the LGBTQ community in both Serbia and Russia has unfortunately remained a mere object rather than subject in the social and political life. In that respect, this article tests the notion of a lack of influence of the said community by examining numerous social and political obstacles that the community has faced in both states so far. In addition, pervasive social norms and values, as well as media coverage of the said community, are included into the analysis presented so as to complement the overall discussion on both cases. The article confirms that the obstacles in the Serbian case have been much smaller than in the case of Russia, particularly when taking into consideration changes in the legal framework regarding functioning of the LGBTQ community in Serbia and their lack in the Russian case, and the comparative findings in this regard are presented in the conclusion.

There are five different sections in the article: the first two discuss the case of Serbia, the following two present the analysis on Russia in the same methodological pattern, whereas the last section is the conclusion where the comparative perspective of the cases analyzed is provided. This article aims to fill the gap in the literature on the topic at hand since there is a considerable lack in this regard. Hence, studies analyzing specifically the issues addressed in this study, to the best of its authors' knowledge, have not yet been published, and thus this article may serve as an invitation for further exploration in this regard. This does not mean that the Serbian and Russian LGBTQ communities and their functioning have not already been addressed in their own terms, but rather that a more comprehensive comparison between the cases has so far not been introduced. Therefore, it would certainly be beneficial to have more insight into the matters at hand, chiefly into the comparative perspective, which would additionally help the whole field of academic literature on the LGBTQ community to develop even further.

Serbia after 1991

Caught in the process of dissolution of the joint Yugoslav state, the Republic of Serbia was from the end of the 1980s to the late 2000s led by an authoritarian regime of Slobodan Milošević whose rule came to coincide with the political, economic, and social downfall of the once relatively prosperous Yugoslav republic. Milošević's authoritarian regime introduced Serbia into a cycle of violence and destruction of civic values, and also brought the country to an edge of economic ruin. With wars raging in neighboring BiH

and Croatia in the early 1990s, the Serbian regime embraced nationalism in order to sustain itself in power. While publicly denouncing involvement in the regional conflicts and voicing strong support to supposed "protection of Serbian nation," the regime effectively introduced Serbian society into a decade where civic values were replaced by introduction of traditional social patterns, based on patriarchal social models that fitted well with the nationalist discourse that was officially promoted. These social models, as Papić wrote back in 1994, reintroduced and reinforced gender inequality in the country, and also influenced those negative social developments that made acceptance of minority communities, such as the LGBTQ, impossible. This refusal of recognition for the LGBTQ minority has, for that matter, roots in those social values and practices that were promoted in both Kingdom of Yugoslavia and Socialist Yugoslavia since, for example, homosexual intercourse was punishable by law "under paragraphs 129.b and 206 of the Penal Code" as "crime against nature" and "under article 186 of the Yugoslav Penal Code" as "unnatural fornication between males" in both states, respectively.

In addition, the Serbian Orthodox Church has also influenced the rise of nationalism in Serbia, supported it so as to gain more influence in the society, and also managed to pose itself as the crucial actor in the political life of the country. Hence, Serbia turned into a sort of a pariah state and its post-socialist development has thus been marked by an extremely negative, in one word anti-European, legacy of Milošević's regime. This being said, it is to be expected that LGBTQ community in Serbia after 1991 has had a very specific development, largely due to the conditions the country found itself in after 1991. Therefore, the LGBTQ community became organized in the beginning of the 1990s, on the eve of destruction of Socialist Yugoslavia, in a rather informal fashion, as Mlađenović wrote back in 2005. She pointed out that members of the Serbian LGBTQ initiated informal meetings and in 1991 in Belgrade formed a group named "Arkadia", which already in 1994, the same year when Serbia actually decriminalized same-sex sexual intercourse, was registered and published its first newsletters. It was actually in the following years that lesbian members of "Arkadia" decided to form a separate organization named "Labris", which was registered, largely due to vague regulations on NGO registration at that time, only in 2000.

War-torn Serbia ruled by the authoritarian regime and built on anti-civic values was definitely no place for any "coming-out" of members of the LGBTQ community. This is the main reason why the community itself remained on the margins of the society in the Milošević era. Hence, although members of this community often engaged in protests against the conflicts in the region and although they sided with those social groups, for example, ethnic minorities, that were mistreated under the regime, their voices remained largely unheard. In that respect, it should come as no wonder that many members of this community, very much like

many young and educated people, left the country during the warring decade. Serbia in the 1990s was no place for those whose value system was different from the one supported by the regime engaged in, what Gordy termed, "destruction of alternatives."

It was only after 2000, following democratic changes in Serbia, that a number of LGBTQ organizations came into existence by "coming out." Today there are more than a dozen such organizations registered in major cities in Serbia, predominantly in Belgrade and Novi Sad as social and cultural hubs. However, there are two sides of this "coming out" coin. On the one hand, it is certain that, as elsewhere in the region caught in post-2000 democratic transition, "grassroots social movements organized by LGBTI individuals, for example, have become visible players in the public spheres" and "an *insistent presence and growth* of civil society organizations for LGBTI rights" has been witnessed. However, and this is the other, the ugly, side of the coin, it is also crucial to note that, regardless of democratic transformation, regime change has not exactly meant the change of anti-civic values and practices. This means that "coming out" of members of the LGBTQ community has meant relatively little in terms of the community's social influence, largely because the Serbian society, mirroring other societies in the region, has remained far from ready to accept members of the LGBTQ community as their equals. Hence, "visible players" have not yet become "influential players," as it will be discussed further on in this article. Pride Parades in Belgrade of 2001 and 2010, and numerous failed attempts between and beyond, have both shown that radical nationalist organizations and ultra-right movements still have the capability, and are effectively allowed, to inflict harm to members of the LGBTQ community, and that, on the other hand, the state of Serbia has in this respect shown very little interest in dealing with causes of this problem.

Speaking from a purely legal standpoint, Serbia has after 2000 made a tremendous move forward in acknowledging the LGBTQ community's existence and rights. However, it is also important to note sluggishness in the process because Serbia is the last state in the region to have adopted legal regulations on anti-discrimination in 2009. In addition, it was only in 2008, exactly 18 years after the respective decision of the World Health Organization, that Medical Association of Serbia removed homosexuality from its list of diseases. "Serbia is a party to the various international and regional human rights conventions which prohibit discrimination against minorities, and has enacted anti-discrimination and hate speech laws," but the LGBTQ community in Serbia is still faced with social stigmatization, largely stemming from patriarchal social notions, and is therefore unable to realize its rights in practice. Hence, speaking in principle, in its Article 21, Serbian Constitution states that "everyone shall have the right to equal legal protection, without discrimination," and Article 387 of the Serbian Criminal Code provides a framework for prosecuting those who threaten or-

ganizations and individuals due to their commitment to the "equality of people." With regard to international law, Serbia is a party to the European Convention on Human Rights ("ECHR") and the International Covenant on Civil and Political Rights ("ICCPR"), both of which prohibit discrimination under the law," but practice is unfortunately different from principle. Legal changes in laws governing media, education, labor, military service, and health insurance all represent important points of progress, but still mean little if not applied in practice.

This is a typical problem for states in transition that suffer from considerable discrepancy between legal regulations and their applications. Hence, this point actually proves that pervasive patriarchal social attitudes and the rather slow process of institutional change have resulted in the relatively slow and protracted acceptance of the LGBTQ community. For example, transnational watchdog groups such as ILGA-Europe document the continuation of anti-LGBTI hate speech across all regions of Europe; as they reported in 2013. "Degrading, offensive, and defamatory language is being used by public officials at all levels—starting from heads of states to local councilors." In addition, mainstream media has been for years providing insufficient attention to the community which "has been continuously *deleted from the texts* of all mainstream media programs". This is still certainly the case and it proves that members of the community, even 14 years after the regime change, are still considered social outcasts. The fact is that, according to a 2013 report, 49% of the Serbian population still views homosexuality as essentially an illness, there is unfortunately considerable prejudice against LGBTQ individuals, and, moreover, other ethnic and minority religious communities are also continually viewed in a prejudiced way. Hence, "authoritarian mentality, political anti-culture, and prejudice," as the Commissioner for Protection of Equality in Serbia said, continue to rule the day in the country where gender gap is considerable and where stereotypes deeply characterize social relations.

"Visible Players" Are Not "Influential Players" in Serbia

As pointed out in the previous section, Serbia has made considerable democratic progress and has also advanced toward respect of LGBTQ rights. However, it seems fair to say that despite substantial breakthroughs, the LGBTQ community still faces huge social obstacles. Therefore, this section of the article is dedicated to discussion on constraints to the said community in Serbia, which obviously still characterize its existence and functioning.

To begin with, speaking from the standpoint of the political and legal framework, "the implementation of laws, policies, and other regulations at the general level" remains the biggest issue. This means that although Serbia itself is in principle dedicated to protecting human rights of the said community, this is in practice an un-

likely case. For example, the verdict of January 2013 against discrimination in the workplace based on sexual orientation is *the first* of its kind to have been reached and was immediately marked as an astounding success in this respect. The 2013 EU Progress Report hence clearly referred to various issues within the rule of law, such as reforming the judiciary, fighting corruption and organized crime, institutional and public administration reform, as well as anti-discrimination and minority protection, as the most significant issues the country needed to improve. This, therefore, proves the point that an already faulty judiciary is ill-prepared, unprofessional, and biased, particularly so toward LGBTQ cases. Hence, as a 2011 report stated, "insufficiently clear political will is a key factor in hindering faster and clearer promotion and implementation of the rights of LGBT population in Serbia. ... Although the law provides for court protection against discrimination, it is most difficult for the members of the LGBT community to obtain effective and adequate protection in a court procedure."

The EU in 2013 reported on this issue and stated that although "some additional efforts were made by the authorities and independent institutions on the protection of other vulnerable groups, in particular of the lesbian, gay, bisexual, transgender and intersex (LGBTI) population, sufficient political support is lacking. It was in particular regrettable that the Pride Parade was banned for the third year in a row on security grounds; this was a missed opportunity to demonstrate respect for fundamental rights." Thus, Serbia needs to ensure respect of individuals in terms of "the right to be free from discrimination based on their sexual orientation or gender identity; the right to be free from cruel and degrading treatment or punishment; the right to a fair trial; the right to recognition before the law and the right to freedom from arbitrary interference with privacy, family, or home; the right to freedom of assembly; and the right to freely-chosen family life." It is, in that sense, impossible for the said community in Serbia to fully realize its rights because the political elite do not engage in a sufficient manner to ensure the respect of the aforementioned rights and hence show only partial commitment in this respect. Therefore, the country *ought* to "use all appropriate means, including criminal prosecutions, against individuals who incite, threaten, and or carry out acts of violence against LGBT individuals and groups," "actively condemn hate crimes against LGBT persons through state institutions, and especially representatives of executive power," and engage in an education campaign, especially designed for public officials at all levels, aimed at providing truthful information about the said community and its rights.

In addition to the problem of law implementation, the LGBTQ community is also faced with a variety of discriminatory social attitudes that are displayed in the media and that are often held and publicly advocated by state officials, political leaders, as well as religious leaders. In that respect, it is important to mention that

these homophobic attitudes and hate speech, built on a stereotype of *normality* as "marked by Serbdom, Orthodox Christianity, tradition and unalterable gender roles, while the countertype— signifying degeneration—encompasses the pro- European orientation, secularism, equality between man and woman and, finally, homosexuality and LGBT rights," play an extremely important role in social life since discourses reflecting homophobic and anti-civic values are in this way created, disseminated, and institutionalized. Hence "the resistance to modernization and homophobic discourse remain and time and again regenerate, which is clearly reflected through the system of value matrix of the younger generations." These attitudes, often delivered in a derogatory emotional language, are aimed at alienating certain social groups by depicting them in a wrongful and untrue manner. It is, therefore, essential for journalists to engage in truthful media coverage of the community since "the freedom of expression also implies responsibility, which is, among other things, regulated by the ethical codes of journalism. It is important that the journalists themselves go through continual education about professional reporting about sensitive social topics" and perform their duty in a professional manner. Speaking, for instance, about the print media alone, the 2013 report states that, although there was a relatively small percentage of articles that "report negatively, discriminatory, by using stereotypical explanations," it remains clear that "LGBT population is still exposed to hate speech and marginalization, even though the neutral contextualization of LGBT topics is dominant in the media discourse. The total number of articles with a neutral position toward the LGBT population is 1,241, which makes it 75.3% of all the articles, although an increase in the number of positive articles in comparison to previous years was also noticed."

In addition, state officials, politicians, and religious leaders should not make public statements that "perpetuate discrimination on the basis of sexual orientation and gender identity." For example, the 2014 flooding in Serbia has been described by Serbian Orthodox Church leaders as "divine punishment" for the LGBTQ community's "vices." In addition to this, politicians often contribute to the anti-homosexual frenzy by, for instance, acting in manner of ex-PM Dačić who publicly refused to "become gay" for the sake of Serbia entering the EU. His public dismissal of the LGBTQ community, depicted in light of the necessity for EU integration, was supposed to hide the state inability and unwillingness to stop those individuals threatening the Pride Parade that should have been held in Belgrade in September 2013. It is clearly the case that although they hold the key to social transformation of the country and although they *should lead* that very transformation toward liberal democracy, the political elite often tend to downplay the importance of human rights of the LGBTQ community and justify this behavior with security reasons. In this way the elite assist anti-civic social discourses and continue to label the LGBTQ community "as moral

and/or physical degeneration constituting a threat to the normal societal order and Serbian nationhood."

Last of all, it should be taken into consideration that the LGBTQ community has indeed become organized in a much better fashion over the years and that "there have been noticeable developments within mainstream politics and culture regarding LGBTI inclusion in Southeast Europe." However, regardless of these positive developments reflecting the community "becoming more visible in the Southeast European region" and the fact that the community's "activists are using the opportunity of the current window of international scrutiny of their countries' practices and policies to press for rights against discrimination and homophobic violence," it is still the case that the political elite in Serbia have not made any serious attempt toward establishing proper channels of cooperation with these organizations. As pointed out by Miletić, Serbia has done very little to include the said organizations in decisions over matters that are of significance to this community, and, in addition, consultation with the political elite happens only in that measure that is required by the EU. This issue may be viewed in light of the importance of civil society organizations in the process of democratic transition toward the EU in general, but unfortunately there is unwillingness of the political elite to establish broader cooperation with civil society in this respect.

This point should not be taken as surprising because the political elite have, on the one hand, shown very little will toward proper law implementation, and, on the other, have often engaged in anti-LGBTQ discourses based on homophobic and anti-civic attitudes. In addition to this, it should also be said that the political elite tend to influence the said organizations by trying to manage their respective agendas in directions suitable to their own goals. Thus, there seems to be no real channel, open and without hindrance, of communication between the two sides. The Serbian political elite obviously have very little interest in the fact that the said organizations possess both experience and capacities that are essential for successful democratization of the country. Hence, the political elite *should* bear in mind that the said community's members can become "potential leaders in changing political realities and actors of the democratization of the society," as training sessions in political leadership held in May 2014 have already shown, but these organizations need to be approached by the aforementioned elite. Activism of the LGBTQ community in media presentations, various public performances, and social media campaigns, being part of both international and domestic civic organizations is certainly very positive for democratization, but the state needs to start playing a more responsible and active role toward inclusion if it truly wants to see the said community become a subject rather than object in domestic politics.

To conclude, it is obvious that Serbian LGBTQ organizations have become more "visible" but still not influential players due to three issues:

first, these organizations face faulty law implementation that constrains them from fully exercising their rights; second, they are still met with negative social attitudes most often presented in the media and disseminated by both political and religious leaders; and, last of all, channels of communication between the political elite and the LGBTQ community remains largely one-sided, with the former trying to influence the said community. Hence, it may be claimed that the said community has remained largely unable to influence social change and thus continues to maneuver in a relatively constrained social space. This social space can only be extended if the elite engage in ensuring proper law implementation, continue to push toward civic values and social institutionalization of respective discourses, and, last of all, establish genuine means of communication and cooperation with the said community.

Russia and LGBTQ: A Historical Retrospective

In February 2013, the Russian non-governmental research organization Levada Analytical Center conducted a survey of public opinion regarding attitudes to homosexuality in light of the infamous and now already adopted law on "Homosexuality Propaganda." Respondents were asked questions related to their attitudes toward homosexuals, nature of homosexuality, as well as questions about the rights of sexual minorities in Russia. The results showed that 34% of respondents believed that homosexuality was a disease to be treated, 23% that homosexuality came out of inappropriate parenting, 17% that homosexuality resulted from sexual abuse, and only 16% were positive in regard to the fact that homosexuality was a sexual orientation. 16% of the same respondents believed that homosexuals should be isolated from society, 27% that they needed to be provided with psychological and other assistance, 22% that they needed medical treatment, and 5% support eliminating the said community. Only 23% agreed that homosexuals should have same rights as the rest of the population.

To have an insight into the LGBTQ issue in Russia today, it is of importance to understand the evolution of the historical and cultural context in relation to homosexuality in Russian society. Pre-Modern Slavic culture (900–1700) "developed generally negative view on sexuality ... and a broad system of constraints on its manifestations in practice. Confession and penitence, as well as numerous regulations about sexual abstinence in marriage, were important instruments in maintaining social stability in the family-based society." The gender roles between men and women were clearly divided and canon law dictated which expressions of sexuality were forbidden, including homosexuality. However, only under the rule of Nicholas I in 1845 *muzhelozhstvo* ("man lying with man") became punishable with deprivation of rights and resettlement in Siberia for up to 5 years. Interestingly so, female homosexuality has never historically been perceived as a crime but rather as a disease that is to be treated. A period of freedom for

Russian homosexuals started with the establishment of the Soviet Union when many previous laws were abolished, with social values, religious views, and many traditions deconstructed. "History has never seen such a variety of personal relationships—indissoluble marriage with its 'stable family', 'free unions', secret adultery; a girl living quite openly with her lover in so-called 'wild marriage'; pair marriage, marriage in threes and even the complicated marriage of four people—not to talk of the various forms of commercial prostitution." Consequently, sexuality and sexual preferences became the private matter of individuals and homosexuality became decriminalized.

Later on, the Stalin regime brought back to life and even reinforced criminalization of homosexuality in 1933. This move was inspired by those negative views of homosexuality as being a problematic trait of aristocracy, bourgeoisie, and foreign elements in the Soviet Union. Article from the "Great Soviet Encyclopedia" characterized homosexuality as a sexual perversion, unnatural attraction to persons of the same sex, and punishable by criminal law for up to 5 years. "Soviet medical authorities and lawyers described homosexuality as a manifestation of "moral decadence of the bourgeoisie." Homosexuality was tied to counter-revolution, and, therefore, became a convenient tool for the next 50 years to target the disobedient and create both fear and respect to the state and those in power. There is no official information on the number of people prosecuted under the notorious Article 121, but it is believed to be about 1,000 people per year. The state hence did everything to de-sexualize public discourses, such as arts and media, and thus, as one renowned quote states just to verify the atmosphere of the time, "there was no sex in USSR."

Despite even being highly criminalized and stigmatized during Soviet times, gays and lesbians continued to be the part of the society but kept their profile low: the LGBTQ community developed its own system of communication through hidden meetings, hidden messages, appropriate slang, and thus created a basis for the movement's existence in the 1990s. Thus, first references to this community, mostly in relation to homosexuality and AIDS, did not appear in the Soviet media till perestroika of the late 1980s. The AIDS epidemic was bound to homosexuality, which was depicted as "a dangerous pathology and was said to be a violation of normal principles of sexual relationships. ... Homosexuality challenges both normal heterosexual relationships and society's cultural, moral attainments ..." Only from 1993 could one talk of decriminalization of homosexuality and relative freedom for the LGBTQ community in Russia since, following suit of a number of other post-communist countries, pressure from the Council of Europe influenced legal changes in this respect. However, decriminalization of homosexuality in the then Russia, very much like in other states caught in post-communist transition, could not automatically produce changes in dominant social attitudes.

Hence, it was from 1993 that Russian LGBTQ individuals, predominantly homosexuals, slowly started "coming out" and organizing themselves in communities. The situation before 2006 in Russia was similar to that of the United States in the early 1990s when "being gay was no longer criminal or shameful, but it was still not a topic for polite conversation or public discussion. Issues such as same-sex marriage or protection from discrimination were not on the table, but then again, Russia was rebuilding itself as a dictatorship, so the political table had been hijacked." It was only in 1999 that both homosexuality and bisexuality were finally removed from the list of diseases when Russia adopted the appropriate WHO classification. However, while homophobia in Russia had a tendency to decline in the 1990s, largely due to political, economic, and social liberalization in the period of intense exchange with the West, the end of the decade signaled changes in this respect. With Putin's rise to power in 2000, marked by a mix of political heavy-handedness with traditional values from both imperial Russian and Soviet times, homophobia has been on the rise in political, social, and cultural spheres of life. Certainly, the more authoritarian approach Putin has favored both in domestic and foreign policy since taking power has also brought re-traditionalization to the Russian society and hence influenced revival of illiberal social attitudes and respective legislation. This, therefore, means that the Russian regime has become engaged in a "witch-hunt" in order to alienate those domestic civil rights groups and organizations viewed as potential threats to the regime. Thus, the regime based on illiberal means has gone into a war with LGBTQ propaganda in order to evade tackling serious social, economic, and political problems in the country.

Therefore, in 2006 the first law banning homosexual propaganda was passed by the Ryazan region, and by 2012 more than 11 regions in total, including the cultural capital of Russia St. Petersburg, followed the same pattern. On the federal level, a law was passed unanimously by the parliament and entered into force on June 30, 2013. The law bans dissemination of "propaganda for nontraditional sexual relationships," labeled as lesbian, gay, and bisexual relationships, among children. The most serious problem in this respect is that the law defines propaganda in an imprecise manner, leaving it "open to interpretation," and an activist for a regional non-profit organization *Coming Out St. Petersburg* stated that "this law is so vaguely formulated ... it's not really possible to know which actions are legal or illegal because nobody knows what this "propaganda" is." According to Human Rights Watch Russia, the "law denies LGBTQ individuals equal social standing and implies that their identities and relationships are unnatural and perverse." In 2013, Putin signed another anti-LGBTQ bill, banning adoption of Russian orphans by same-sex couples or by single people and/or unmarried couples from countries that permit same-sex marriage. The bill that became law during the Olympic Games in 2014 raised an international outrage

over the Russian government's actions and domestically influenced considerable rise in anti-LGBTQ sentiments. Hence, politicians and government officials have been witnessed on a number of occasions equalizing LGBTQ individuals with pedophiles and have often engaged in hate speech without any fear of being prosecuted in courts of law. This is the reason why LGBTQ individuals, organizations, and advocates for LGBTQ rights have been abused in numerous ways, often fired from their jobs, threatened, and morally and physically attacked. The grimmest issue is, however, that this could be only the beginning of a new LGBTQ criminalization wave, including revoking parents' rights, re-criminalizing same-sex relations, and changes to the Russian constitution to define marriage as union of two heterosexual individuals.

(In)Visible LGBTQ Activism in Russia: Features, Challenges, and Future Perspectives

According to Sozaev, LGBTQ movement in Russia is a part of the international LGBTQ movement, but with its own development path characterized by three waves in evolution. The early 1990s were marked by liberalization and decriminalization of homosexuality. The period between the end of the 1990s and 2005 was noted for the birth of internet activism and establishment of quality web platforms for networking and communication between LGBTQ individuals in Russia (such as gay.ru, lesbiru.com, and similar). Last but not least, the period after 2005/2006 can be associated with "coming out", and the emergence of two influential activist groups: GAYRUSSIA and Russian LGBT-network. As reported by Lapina, there is no internal unity within the community: there are different activist groups with different ideologies and methods situated in different parts of the country. Initially, LGBTQ activism was mainly present in Moscow and Sankt Petersburg, while other regions have witnessed a relatively slow rise of local LGBTQ communities. Different views on official state policies toward the community have influenced internal divisions and hence the movement has become divided between radicals and moderates. Radical activists place emphasis on political aspects; they are more aggressive in both action and statement, and engage in protests and rallies. Moderate activists, however, aim to inform the population on homosexuality through educational programs, social advocacy, public campaigns, and the like. Inner lack of unity and collaboration prevents the community from developing a common strategy, shared goals, and a more unified public profile.

However, it is not the differences in the said community but rather the following obstructions that impede it in Russia. First of all, the official position of the Russian state is discriminatory. Although Moscow denies discrimination, practice has proved otherwise. Despite the Human Rights Commissioner stating that all citizens, regardless of gender, race, religion, or belief are guaranteed legal protection and President Putin saying that homosexuals "face no discrimination at work or in society," the legal framework supposedly protecting traditional cultural and moral values of the society points in an opposite direction. Therefore, according to a 2014 report, Russia's "intense concerted efforts to limit the human rights of LGBTI people reached an all-time high. The executive, legislative and judiciary branches of government; religious leaders; TV, radio, print and online media; federal, regional and local politicians; and various civil society actors including parent groups or violent nationalists united in restricting the rights of LGBTI people and their supporters (particularly their right to freedom of assembly, expression and association), and framing LGBTI individuals as outcasts." Therefore, equality and nondiscrimination, protection from bias-motivated speech and violence, freedom of assembly, association and expression, and asylum remain problematic issues for Moscow.

In addition, there is no legal framework to entail measures against hate crimes and hate speech since the existing judicial and supervisory practice tends to justify, for instance, hate speech with religious traditions and social values of the society. Thus, attempts to bring to book those guilty of hate speech end in failure since the LGBTQ community is not recognized as a legitimate social group in need of state protection. For example, the governor of the Tambovskaya region in 2008 dismissed claims in a hate speech case by saying: "Tolerance?! It can go to hell! Gays should be torn apart and their parts scattered! This garbage-can should be cleaned!" Very much the same is true for freedom of association, expression, and peaceful assembly, since there have been instances of multiple violations, for example, in cases of rejection of registration of the LGBTQ organizations, prohibition of gatherings, and the like. For instance, "in 2011 four LGBT organizations were denied in their request for official registration in Moscow." The organizers of an international human rights festival also "encountered with an aggressive opposition on behalf of religious and nationalist organizations—up to bodily injures, while the police did not interfere with the incident." Moscow Gay Pride was banned for 100 years by the City Council with explanation that this event would cause "public disorder and that most Muscovites do not support such an event." Various incidents where both individuals and organized groups (vigilantes) have engaged in violence against the LGBTQ community have been witnessed over the years and it is often the case that authorities do not pursue legal actions against perpetrators.

Moreover, the position of the LGBTQ community is further complicated by the Orthodox Church and its prominent social position and influence. The "Orthodox Church outlasted the official atheism of the Soviet Union and now, after almost a century in the wilderness, has regained most of the power and prestige it enjoyed under the Romanovs." As "The Basis of the Social Concept of the Russian Orthodox Church" explains, the position of the Church towards homosexuality is "that the divinely established marital

union of man and woman cannot be compared to the perverted manifestations of sexuality. ... While treating people with homosexual inclinations with pastoral responsibility, the Church is resolutely against the attempts to present this sinful tendency as a "norm" and even something to be proud of and emulate." Head of Moscow Patriarchate's department for external relations has claimed that homosexuality "leads to creating an increasing number of same-sex unions who claim to be marriages, while it goes without saying that such unions do not produce posterity. The destruction of traditional family ideals leads to a considerable decrease in the number of extended families."

Hence, there is obviously a close resemblance between the official state and Church views. Moreover, knowing that the influence of the Church has been rising since the 1990s, it should not come as surprising that it today represents an important element in the way Russian society sees and identifies itself. Therefore, "being Orthodox and being Russian are one and the same" and "the Russian Orthodox Church has re-branded itself as the repository of Russian patriotism." This is a very important point to remember in the discussion on the LGBTQ community because the Church has fully agreed with and supported the state policies of re-traditionalization of values, and has also been largely acquiescent with the increasingly authoritarian political direction Moscow has taken. The "Church and the Russian government are in a marriage of convenience. The Russian Orthodox Church is given free rein to try to change social mores through public institutions like the media, films, the military, and the educational curriculum. In return, the government gets the support of what President Medvedev in February 2011 called 'the largest and most authoritative social institution in contemporary Russia.'" This is the consequence of increasing ties between the Church and the state because "Mr. Putin's policies have also taken a sharply conservative turn since his return to the Kremlin last year for a third term as President. Once viewed as a liberal, Mr. Putin has in the past 12 months embraced the church's positions on such sensitive issues as abortion and gay rights." Not only that this direction has served Putin politically by augmenting his power, it has also allowed him to create a specific *macho* image of a modern Russian seen as a defender of Russian values and way of life. "Many people came to see queer visibility (and other liberal manifestations) as a symptom, if not the cause, of economic and social disaster. In the affective politics of today, Putin's 'manhood' and his readiness to take tough action are inextricably and smartly connected to the promise of economic and social stability for the country."

Last of all, the media have also played an increasingly important role in anti-LGBTQ propaganda and have effectively helped discriminatory social discourses. Instead of aiming to provide objective accounts, state-run media, more than any other, tend to side with the official state position in this respect. There are, of course, opposition voices, but it is certain that their influence

is seriously limited, chiefly because the state has generally aimed to curb opposition views. "The discriminatory impact of the anti-LGBT law and hateful language on state television have created a climate of intolerance against the Russian LGBT community," and the state "should denounce, not feed, homophobic hysteria, or the Kremlin's silence will be taken as condoning the violence." An organization-monitoring media called Medialogiya has reported that "the number of news reports referring to homosexuality on official TV channel **Rossiya 1** has skyrocketed over the past few years. In 2011, there were just 11, whereas in 2013 there were more than 160."

In addition to the state-run media, it is quite common for various public figures to express discriminatory attitudes. Thus, state "officials, journalists, and celebrities" "have publicly called LGBT people 'perverts', 'sodomites', and 'abnormal', and have conflated homosexuality with pedophilia." These biased attitudes have had a profound impact by introducing a completely false image of the said community and have also assisted in promoting negative views, making the community a convenient target for prejudice. In addition, there is a need for establishing a constructive dialogue between the LGBTQ organizations and the media since there is no trust between the two sides. This is quite understandable considering the problems that the community has experienced so far. This state of affairs explains why the said community, fearing exposure with potentially disastrous consequences, still keeps its doors closed to the media. Unfortunately, this is precisely the consequence of negative political and social developments in previous years since today's Russian society shows, as Dubrovsky pointed out, very little solidarity for human rights and almost no understanding that every human rights violation is in fact violation of each and everybody's human rights *per se*.

In sum, the LGBTQ community in Russia today faces great obstacles. It is obvious that negative perceptions of the said community advocated by the media and public figures, absence of social will to understand "the otherness," and political constraints without any doubt lead to social stigmatization. Nowadays, when homophobia has in fact become the official state position, the LGBTQ community has to search for new strategies to survive and defend its rights. Transformation of the existing social mindset and respective practices is thus necessary if the invisible and powerless LGBTQ community is to fight for any social change.

Conclusion:
A Comparative Perspective

With respect to the previously presented arguments in both cases and in order to conclude in a comparative manner, it may be said that it is, on the one hand, certain that Serbia has witnessed a more positive change in respect of the LGBTQ community's rights in general. While Russia has over the last couple of years, following an overall authoritari-

an political direction, introduced broad legal restraints toward the LGBTQ community and has thus limited space for social change in this respect, Serbia has noted positive developments in its legal framework by allowing the said community to, at least in principle, enjoy rights that it is obviously denied in Russia. However, Serbia has yet to reach that point where its legal framework is actually fully exercised, since it suffers from a considerable discrepancy between principle and practice. As for Russia, it may be said that the Kremlin has seriously tightened its anti-LGBTQ laws and introduced its LGBTQ community into a citizenship of essentially a lower class. This, in practice, means that the aforementioned community in Russia is in essence outlawed and in both principle and practice discriminated against.

In addition, regardless of the differences when it comes to the legal framework, what seems to bind both Serbia and Russia together to a certain degree are discriminatory attitudes of political figures, religious leaders (chiefly Orthodox Church dignitaries), and certain media outlets toward the LGBTQ community. Russia, however, represents a more extreme case in this regard chiefly due to an uncompromising attitude of its political elite, a considerably higher social influence of its Orthodox Church, the extent of both individual and group violence staged against the LGBTQ community, and negative state-run media coverage of the said community. The Serbian political elite has, on the other hand, been at least in principle dedicated to the EU integration process and this has therefore resulted in its treatment of the LGBTQ community to be much more tolerant. More than that, the Serbian Orthodox Church has not been as influential as the Russian Church, and its ties with the political elite have not been as extensive as in the Russian case.

Last but not least, regardless of Serbia being more liberal than Russia in terms of acceptance of civic values in general, it should be kept in mind that anti-civic and anti-European values have not completely disappeared from Serbian public discourse and have in turn, very much as in the Russian case, inspired sporadic violent acts against members of the LGBTQ community. It is, however, true that these incidents have happened on a smaller scale than in the case of Russia. The fact remains, that the said community is still publicly discriminated against in both states by individuals with political and social influence who should be advancing the agenda of tolerance rather than that of apartheid on the basis of sexual preference. Hence, there are obviously numerous political and religious leaders in both states who refuse to recognize the existence and human rights of the LGBTQ community, while organized groups, such as vigilantes, ultra-right organizations, and the like, have staged attacks on LGBTQ individuals. This state of affairs needs to be taken into serious consideration and it is the political elite that have an enormous responsibility in this regard, whereby ensuring respect of LGBTQ rights should represent a major concern; otherwise no social progress shall be achieved.

"There's No Thing as a Whole Story": Storytelling and the Healing of Sexual Violence Survivors among Women and Girls in Acoliland, Northern Uganda

Oluwaseun Bamidele

Institute of Peace, Security and Governance, Ekiti State University, Ado-Ekiti, Nigeria. kaybamk@gmail.com

Abstract

Storytelling has become an important and acceptable tool among academics and professional peace-builders. Storytelling can be therapeutic, especially since it assists survivors and the society in transition to come to terms with a traumatic past. It has been included as a part of transitional justice mechanisms which have assisted in the area of truth-finding and accountability. It has been useful for peace-building in communities that are deeply rooted in conflict and, therefore, has been encouraged within the last decade in a number of countries around the world. Consequently, this paper is a critical exploration of the discursive links between sexual violence and storytelling in war and peace. The focus is on Acoli women and girls in Acoliland, northern Uganda, who have primarily been impacted by the Lord's Resistance Army (LRA) group of Joseph Kony. Their stories of trauma, resilience, and courage in the face of terror have not been properly acknowledged. Using women and girls of the Acoli community in northern Uganda as an example, this paper aims to begin a discussion on the role of storytelling in the healing of sexual violence survivors. Informed by the storytelling discourse, the paper argues that constructive storytelling exercises can provide an avenue for survivors of sexual violence to acknowledge trauma, attain healing, build resilience, and counter the violent narrative of the group. However, this study also finds that storytelling as a peace-building tool falls short of transforming gender relations. Finally, the paper proposes and designs a storytelling program.

Keywords: *Sexual violence; Storytelling; Survivors; Violent narrative; Northern Uganda*

摘要

讲故事已成为学者和专业和平建设者所接受的重要工具。说故事有治疗的作用，尤其是当它协助幸存者和过渡时期的社会一起去接受过去的创伤。　它同时也属于一种过渡司法机制，帮助寻找真相和问责。它能帮助深陷于冲突中的社区建立和平，因此在过去十年里许多国家都鼓励使用该方法。本文对战争与和平中性暴力和说故事之间存在的"话语连接"（discursive link）进行了重要探索。本文聚焦于生活在乌干达北部地区的阿乔利妇女和女孩，她们基本上都被约瑟夫·科尼（Joseph Kony）领导的圣主抵抗军（Lord's Resistance Army，简称LRA）欺凌。许多故事都有关于她们遭遇的创伤、坚韧和面对恐惧时的勇气，但这些故事却还没有受到正确的认识。通过将她们故事作为例子，本文致力于讨论说故事在治愈性暴力幸存者时产生的作用。在了解说故事话语之后，本文认为："构造性说故事"（constructive storytelling）能为性暴力幸存者提供一条途径，进而接受创伤、获得治愈、建立忍耐并反抗暴力叙事。然而，本文还发现：说故事作为一种建立和平的工具却还无法转变性别关系。最后，本文提出并设计了一项说故事计划。

关键词： 性暴力；讲故事；幸存者；暴力叙事；乌干达北部

Resumen

La narración de historias se ha convertido en una herramienta importante entre académicos y activistas de paz. La narración de cuentos puede ser terapéutica, especialmente al ayudar a los sobrevivientes y la sociedad en transición a enfrentarse a un pasado traumático. La narración se ha incluido como una parte de los mecanismos de justicia transicional que han ayudado en la búsqueda de la verdad y la adjudicación de responsabilidades. También ha sido útil para la construcción de la paz en comunidades que han estado inmersas en conflictos y que, por ende, han sido promovidas en la última década numerosos países alrededor del mundo. Por consiguiente, este artículo propone una exploración crítica de los enlaces discursivos entre la violencia sexual y la narración en momentos de guerra y paz. El enfoque será en las mujeres y niñas acholi, en Acoliland, al norte de Uganda quienes han sido agredidas por el Ejército de Resistencia del Señor (LRA, por sus siglas en inglés), liderado por Joseph Kony. Sus historias del trauma, la resiliencia y el coraje frente al terror no han sido suficientemente reconocidas. Al usar como ejemplo a las niñas y mujeres de la comunidad acholi del norte de Uganda, este artículo intenta inaugurar una discusión acerca del papel de la narración en la sanación de las sobrevivientes de violencia sexual. Teniendo en cuenta el discurso de la narración, este artículo arguye que los ejercicios de narración constructiva pueden proveer una vía de reconocimiento del trauma, construcción de resiliencia para los sobrevivientes de la violencia sexual, y contrarrestar de esta manera la narrativa violenta del grupo. Sin embargo, este estudio también reconoce la insuficiencia de la narración como constructora de paz al momento de transformar las relaciones de género. Finalmente, este artículo propone y diseña un programa de narración.

Palabras clave: *Violencia Sexual, Narración, Sobrevivientes, Violencia Narrativa, Norte de Uganda*

Introduction

Women and girls are particularly vulnerable to sexual violence and rape in situations of armed conflict. Sexual violence and rape against women and girls are often used to dominate, to terrorize, and to humiliate individuals and communities. During armed conflict, women and girls are sexually tortured and abused, which leads to devastating physical and psychological trauma. Rates of sexual violence and rape in Acoliland illustrate that the region is still struggling with a culture of disparity, violence, and patriarchy. The United Nations identified sexual violence and rape as one of the most prominent problems in northern Uganda. From independence in 1962 to date, Uganda has had nine different heads of state with varying tenures. Dr. Milton Obote, who received the instruments of power from the British at independence, became the first president with executive powers and set the trend for the future leaderships. In a sense, he became the mentor of the presidents who succeeded him, including Idi Amin and Yoweri Museveni. Milton Obote (from Lango), Idi Amin (from Kakwa, which is another Nilotic group like the Acoli), Bazilio Olara-Okello and Tito Okello Lutwa (from Acoli), who all hailed from northern Uganda served as heads of state for a total of 21 years between them—a length of time that has only been surpassed by Museveni's ongoing rule. The significant turning point in the development of the leadership in Uganda, into a manipulative one, came in 1967, when Obote abrogated the independence constitution and introduced the republican constitution (commonly referred to as the "pigeon-hole constitution") which granted the president the means to exercise his executive powers according to his whim (Odongo 2003).

Consequently, the advent of manipulative politics paved the way for the rise of armed conflicts in the country. Since it began in 1986, the armed conflict in northern Uganda has gone through various stages and transformations, with several groups emerging to fight the government of Lieutenant General Yoweri Kaguta Museveni. They have included the soldiers of the former Uganda National Liberation Army (UNLA) (the army formed to oust the Idi Amin regime); the Uganda People's Democratic Army (UPDA) led by the late Brigadier Odong Latek; the Holy Spirit Mobile Forces (HSMF) led by a prophetess, the late Alice Auma Lakwena (who died in February 2007 in a refugee camp in Kenya); the Holy Spirit Movement II (HSM II) led by Alice's father, Severino Lukoya; and the Uganda Christian Democratic Army (UCDA), led by Joseph Kony, which changed its name in 1991 to the Lord's Resistance Army (LRA) and is still active, with devastating consequences (Behrend 1998).

As a movement, the LRA's founding is very loosely related to the ongoing power struggle between northern Uganda and the southern provinces near the capital, Kampala. However, the tactics of the LRA defy its occasional proclamation that it is fighting for the independence of the Acoli people, the largest ethnic group in northern Uganda. The LRA attacks Acoli civilians more often than it launches campaigns against the Ugandan government. The LRA's raids on Acoli villages and displacement camps serve to restock the forces with supplies and food (the LRA commonly loots villages before destroying them) as well as with children kidnapped by soldiers. The attacks serve an even more sinister purpose, as the LRA uses its raids as a means of exerting control over the Acoli population by creating a constant state of fear. Common LRA tactics used to instill such fear include mutilation by cutting off lips, ears, and breasts; rape and forced pregnancy; and forced conscription of children. Since 2002, the LRA has abducted an estimated 12,000 children, who have then been subjected to or forced to witness or commit atrocities that compel them to remain with the LRA as fighters, porters, or "wives" (Human Rights Watch 2003). The intensity of the conflict has fluctuated during the past two decades, with the most recent increase in violence occurring in the last 2 years. By all indications, the LRA is now based in the brush forests between southern Sudan and northern Uganda, and has exponentially increased its attacks and the abduction of children. In April 2002, there were an estimated 450,000 displaced people in northern Uganda and most of the total population of the three provinces that constitute Acolil-and-Gulu—Lira, Kitgum, and Pader—have been displaced (UNHCR 2003).

As Dolan (2011) reveals, many survivors of sexual violence and rape in northern Uganda live with the experience of multiple traumas, as a result of having experienced violence themselves, having witnessed it in their family or community and having lost property and their homes. Sexual violence and rape have acute physical, psychological, and social consequences for those who experience and witness it. Sexual violence and rape survivors experience deep psychological trauma, depression, terror, guilt, shame, and loss of self-esteem. Survivors of sexual violence are more likely to be at an increased risk of abuse later in life, are more likely to engage in unprotected sex, and have multiple partners to abuse substances.

Considering the plights of survivors of sexual violence and rape, and the silence surrounding their situation in Acoliland, this paper aims to begin a discussion on the role of storytelling in the healing of survivors of sexual violence and rape. Informed by the storytelling discourse, this paper argues that constructive storytelling exercises can provide an avenue for survivors of sexual violence and rape to acknowledge trauma, attain healing, build resilience, and counter the violent narrative of the group. A storytelling exercise is proposed in the paper: institution-based storytelling program. This paper is structured in four parts. The first part briefly examines what category of people fit into the label of "sexual violence survivors." The second part conceptualizes the storytelling approach and reviews its strengths and weaknesses. The third part presents several stories of survivors of sexual violence and rape. The final part proposes a possible storytelling program for the healing of sexual violence and rape survivors in Acoliland: the institution-based program.

Who are the Survivors of Sexual Violence?

There is no common definition for survivors of sexual violence. The oft-cited definition is provided by the United Nations Special Rapporteur on systematic rape, sexual slavery, and slavery-like practices in armed conflict cited in Watts and Zimmerman. Watts and Zimmerman (2002) define "sexual violence" as:

> ... any violence, physical or psychological, carried out through sexual means or by targeting sexuality, thus including both physical and psychological attacks directed at a person's sexual characteristics, such as forcing a person to strip naked in public, mutilating a person's genitals or slicing of a woman's breasts as well as situations in which two victims are forced to perform sexual acts on one another or to harm one another in a sexual manner. (Watts and Zimmerman 2002)

Article 1 of the 1993 UN Declaration on the Elimination of Violence against Women offered the first official definition of sexual violence as follows:

> ... the term "violence against women" means any act of gender-based violence that results in, or is likely to result in, physical, sexual or psychological harm or suffering to women, including threats of such acts, coercion or

arbitrary deprivation of liberty, whether occurring in public or in private life. (United Nations, Declaration on the Elimination of Violence against Women 1993)

Based on the above definition, the programmatic package uses the term sexual violence:

Sexual violence (SV) is the general term used to capture violence that occurs as a result of the normative role expectations associated with each gender, along with the unequal power relationships between the two genders, within the context of a specific society. (Okello and Hovil 2007)

While women, girls, men, and boys can be survivors of sexual violence, it has been widely acknowledged that the majority of persons affected by sexual violence are women and girls, as a result of an unequal distribution of power in society between women and men. Further, women and girls survivors who are victims of sexual violence suffer specific consequences as a result of gender discrimination. As summed up by United Nations Children's Fund:

The primary targets of sexual violence are women and girls, but not only are they at high risk of sexual violence, they also suffer exacerbated consequences as compared with what men endure. As a result of gender discrimination and their lower

socio-economic status, women have fewer options and less resource at their disposal to avoid or escape abusive situations and to seek justice. They also suffer (...) consequences [on their sexual and reproductive health], including forced and unwanted pregnancies, unsafe abortions and resulting deaths, traumatic fistula, and higher risks of sexually transmitted infections (STIs) and HIV. (UNICEF 2012)

Considering that the LRA armed group victimize "not only the direct survivors but also entire communities or entire nations by spreading fear through sexual violence" (Akumu, Amony, and Otim 2005). The United Nations Children's Fund (2012) broadens the categorization of sexual violence victims to include all civilians, and the society as a whole "who are indiscriminately targeted regardless of their status or function, or public institutions." There are a number of issues at stake in determining who constitutes a survivor of sexual violence. For instance, who puts the label on survivors, and how legitimate is such labeling? In addition, the notion of "survivor" may take away agency from the people who have survived the violent acts of the LRA. For this purpose, the paper will use the label of "survivors" to acknowledge the resilience and agency of those that have been affected by the LRA rebel group in Acoliland, northern Uganda. The following section conceptualizes the storytelling approach and examines its strengths and limitations.

Conceptualization of Storytelling

Storytelling awakens us to that which is real. Honest. It is the most pure form of communication because it transcends the individual. The Kalahari Bushmen have said, "A story is like the wind. It comes from a far-off place, and we feel it." Those things that are the most personal are most general, and are, in turn, most trusted. Stories bind. They are connective tissues. They are basic to who we are. (Chaitin 2003)

Stories are means of constructing stories in the mind, or storytelling—as it has been called—is one of the most fundamental means of making meaning, as such it is an activity that pervades all aspects of learning. When storytelling becomes overt and is given expression in words, the resulting stories are one of the most effective ways of making one's own interpretation of events and ideas available to others. Through the exchange of stories, therefore, people involved can share their understanding of a topic and bring their mental modes of the world into closer alignment. In this sense, stories and storytelling are relevant in all areas of sexual violence (Chaitin 2003). While telling and performing stories, all ideas must be heard, considered, compared, interpreted, and acted upon. The bridges built in a play are lengthened, and their partially exposed signposts are organized and labeled in ways that commit the storyteller to travel in particular directions. The subject encompasses all of language and thought. It is the academic inheritor of the creative wisdom of a play (Chaitin 2003).

Burk (1997) also emphasizes support for this view when he argues that storytelling develops positive and necessary skills in the area of social responsibility: self- and cultural awareness, recognition of social roles, increased communication skills, and opportunity for reflection. Hilder (2005) quotes the influential anthropologist Levi-Strauss when she describes stories as a kind of thinking tool due to their "power ... to fix affective responses to the messages". Storytelling connects our emotions and emotions help us to remember (Hilder 2005; Goodman 2008). Hutchinson (1999) claims "stories, like persons, originate alogically". Owing to this "alogical" origin, the diverse forms of storytelling must be honored and acknowledged (Nicholson and Nicholson 2005). While there is a familiar dominant (patriarchal) story structure existing in Western culture (with a beginning, middle, and end), others exist as well; denying these alternative voices is denying the teller himself/herself, to exclude alternative ways of being (King 2003; Nicholson and Nicholson 2005). Hutchinson (1999) recognizes the existence of diverse story forms when she highlights a story's accommodating qualities: they have the ability to hold at once all of the "ambiguities, contradictions, and breaks in meaning that occur in a life." Such accommodation does not always occur in linear, logical, and climactic order. For Hilder (2005), storytelling must be approached with the intention to "deconstruct exclusivity and invent inclusivity." This involves exposure to and experience with myriad forms and structures of story. Dyson and Genishi (1994) illuminate the risk of not allowing "inappropriate" stories such as those of toughness, violence, abuse, or exploitation.

Through stories, Simmons (2006) contends that "societies and groups create, recreate, and alter social identities, power relations, knowledge, memory, and emotion." Stories "influence our ability to recall events, motivate people to act, modulate our emotional reactions to events, cue certain heuristics and biases, structure our problem-solving capabilities, and ultimately perhaps even constitute our very identity" (Simmons 2006). Storytelling also "include(s) a temporal ordering of events and an effort to make something out of those events; to render, or to signify, the experiences of persons in flux in a personally and culturally coherent, plausible manner" (Simmons 2006). During a storytelling exercise, "events are selected and then given cohesion, meaning, and direction" (Burk 1997). Telling a story could be done through a variety of means, including oral, written, gestures, images, paintings, theatre, music, documentary, film, and drawings. The choice of the medium and method used in telling stories depends on the societal context and the preferences of the storyteller and, perhaps, on the needs and cognitive abilities of the listener(s).

Stories are easily told and disseminated through the media outlet (Barton and Booth 2000). Stories could be told either chronologically or un-chronologically. In other words, the notion of time and sequences of events are essential to the act of storytelling. When recounting experiences, survivors of sexual violence and rape often begin their narrative from the period before the crisis (when things were normal), then narrate their actual experience of the violence, and conclude by sharing experiences of grief, trauma, and grievances after the violent events (Chaitin 2003). Quite aside from the notion of time, stories are told within a specific context or setting. The effectiveness of a storytelling exercise may depend on the kind of atmosphere and space wherein it occurs. The context in which stories are told "influences what, how, and why elements within the story are seen as important and relevant" (Daemmrich 2003). Closely related to the notion of context is that of the audience. According to Miller (1996), the minds of the audience "are the canvas on which storytellers paint their narratives." Sogol (2014) argues that the role of the audience is to identify with the storyteller in a manner that will touch their hearts and lead them to transformative action.

Storytelling and the Recovery of Sexual Violence Survivors

Telling one's story brings to consciousness experiences and events that may have been buried in the pursuit of forgetting. Intrusive memory and forgetting are passive, often experienced as a loss of control. In a supportive context, narrative becomes an active decision. Narrative can be empowering when the individual decides how and where they are willing to share memories (Brison 2002). From Brison's own experience with the narrative act of remembering, he explains, "traumatic memories feel as though they are passively endured, narratives are the result of certain obvious choices" (Brison 2002). Survivors are often taught by their perpetrators and or community to not acknowledge the abuse, to forget their experience, or to believe that their experience does not constitute abuse. This makes the act of remembering and retelling all the more important. Narratives can therefore be seen as an active way of regaining control of one's memory, and recognizing the perpetrator's actions as wrong.

Through narrative, survivors of sexual violence and rape can transform their relationship with their memory of trauma. As Herman (1997) posits: "Remembering and telling the truth about terrible events are prerequisites both for the restoration of the social order and for the healing of sexual violence and rape survivors." In theory, survivors of sexual violence and rape are able to reclaim their own humanity and establish a connection to and control over their own life story. As a conscious act of remembering, sexual violence and rape survivors are able to use narrative to integrate the experience of past trauma into a larger life story. Narrative provides an avenue for human connection. As discussed earlier on in this essay,

trauma is relational. Similarly, narrative is inherently relational. Narrative requires an audience, providing a witness or witnesses to the act of telling one's story. Brison (2002) explains that "in order to construct self-narratives we need not only the words with which to tell our stories, but also an audience able and willing to hear us and to understand our words as we intend them." Yet, the audience or witness can take many different forms, influencing the questions that are asked, how the narrative is formed, and the way in which the story is heard. Watts (1992) explains "the idea of framing the speaking of memories as storytelling is then directly aimed at the release of such emotions through a collective process of narrating life experiences." As a collective process, narrative allows survivors of sexual violence and rape to discover that they are not alone and they are not at fault. This reduces the burden of self-blame and isolation. Uncovering similarities and overlap among the stories, survivors of sexual violence and rape are able to reconstruct their own identity in relation to others. The telling of a survivor's personal story can be employed to reconstruct the past, providing consideration and potential healing for the individual's current identity.

Storytelling also has the potential to transform broken relationships among survivors of sexual violence and rape and groups in a community that is recovering from armed conflict or war. As Sogol (2014) notes, through the act of telling their stories, survivors of sexual violence and rape "engage in a dialectic way, with their past and also exchange information and perspectives, externalize grief, loss, and anger, and try to reach some form of consensus as to a way forward." In addition, storytelling creates "a familiar learning space, a safe space, a communal space, an empowering space, and an imaginative space" for sexual violence survivors (Sogol 2014). These spaces instill confidence, courage, and create understanding and transformational dialogue among survivors of sexual violence and their community members. In Herman's work, narrative is associated with reconstructing the trauma story, and restoring connections between survivors of sexual violence and their community (Herman 1997). Through narrative, survivors of sexual violence and rape piece together their past, and in this process they connect with others. In her work on trauma recovery among survivors of sexual abuse, Herman (1997) describes "the fundamental stages of recovery are establishing safety, reconstructing the trauma story, and restoring the connection between survivors of sexual violence and their community." In Chaitin's view, the public/private dichotomy reveals "an important perspective that is often reflected in survivors of sexual violence and rape testimony, namely, personal and corporate pain" (Chaitin 2003).

Collective sharing of corporate pain could be much easier for survivors of sexual violence and rape. An advantage of the collective sharing of trauma is that it empowers people with common adversity, and as the narrative "evolves from personal stories to a group story, the narrative gains potency

... The new group narrative becomes a new framework for thought and blueprint for action" (Chaitin 2003). At the same time, when survivors share their private experience with the public, they transform their situation from a "narrative of shame and embarrassment to a narrative of witnessing" (Chaitin 2003). Once a "story has been made public, the person who tells it can regain further agency and possibly work toward reconciliation" (Miller 1996). Sharing and integrating one's experiences of trauma with that of others are the empowering aspects of storytelling, and in "recounting one's own story, one salvages and reaffirms, in the face of dispersal, defeat, and death, the social bonds that bind one to a community of kindred souls" (Odongo 2003).

The Narratives of Sexual Violence Survivors

The narratives of survivors of rape and other forms of sexual violence reveal that many still suffer the effects of psychological trauma, as well as discrimination and stigma from the community. Many of the women and girls who suffered sexual violence were interviewed by the author. They were still highly traumatized and were in need of psychological responses in sharing their stories in a well-organized program with the public.

Joanna (14 years old) and Alice (13 years old) in Kitgum narrated their ordeal as follows:

On our way home; we met two LRA rebels at a junction in the

road. The LRA rebels told us to sit on the ground. Then they asked if we have chickens at home. Alice replied in the affirmative, and one LRA rebel then said, "If they are there, let's go and get them." At a certain point, one LRA rebel stopped and began to prepare the ground, stepping on the grass. According to Joanna, He said to us to sit down and then ordered us to take off our clothes. First we refused, and one of the LRA rebel said that if we didn't, he would shoot us. Then he told us to lie down. When Alice [her cousin] didn't, one of the soldiers kicked her in the chest. The darker LRA rebel took Alice a short distance away, while the other one stayed with me. He threatened me with a gun and raped me. I was just crying. The other LRA rebel raped Alice. Then the darker LRA rebel who had raped Alice called me to him and raped me too, while the other one raped Alice. It is the time we need to let the world know what we have passed through.[1]

In another story in Pader, a female survivor named Evelyn (15 years old) narrated her ordeal as follows:

LRA raped many women and some of them were taken and [they] never came back. We don't even know what happened to them, maybe they became wives. Some who came back had children and they told us they were everyone's wife, any man in the jungle could be their husband and the women had no choice. I wish to tell and share my story with the next generation if the Ugandan government can give me the opportunity.[2]

A female survivor in Gulu, Victoria, a 16-year-old girl who was kidnapped, narrated her experience in the LRA camp:

Sexual and domestic violence was common because of the congestion in the camp and thus people used to conflict amongst them[selves] in homes and in the community. ... they used to tell us not to walk at night because you can meet the rebels and they rape or kill you. It happened to me when I was trying to move to another village but it was during the day and I met them with two other women and they raped all of us and then told us to run or we will be dead. I was too weak to run but I tried. My story is yet to be shared for people to hear but if I can have the venue to share my story the government of Uganda can have better programme for us in Acoliland.[3]

---

1 Interview with survivor, Kitgum district, December 3–21, 2012 (name changed to protect identity).

2 Interview with survivor, Kitgum district, December 3–21, 2012 (name changed to protect identity).

3 Interview with survivor, Pader district, December 3–21, 2012 (name changed to protect identity).

Discussion with Akullo, a 13-year-old female survivor in Pader, revealed that:

... without any delay, he started demanding for sex forcefully while pulling my clothes until he made it. After raping and defiling me I decided to have him as my husband. I lived with him for two years and gave birth to two children but later on he started mistreating me. We used to over quarrel and fight in the house. I also want to share my story for the next generation to learn about my ordeal and if the government can organize a program for those of us that we are passing through this situation, the Acoli society will be a better place to live.[4]

Another survivor, Janet was abducted from a secondary school in Pader when she was 15 years old and she spent 5 years in captivity. She said:

I was given to John Okech, one of (LRA leader Joseph) Kony's senior commanders. I was his fourth wife. He soon brought in four other young girls. They were to become his wives when they were slightly older. In the meantime, they were told to baby-sit for his other wives. When you are given a commander as your husband, you are expected to produce food. You are also given a gun and expected to fight. I was often picked to go out on patrols. I became pregnant in early 2002, when Kony predicted an attack from the UPDF on our bases in Sudan. By June, our whole group [had] sneaked back into Uganda and hid in the Imatong mountains. This was the most difficult time for captives. My husband was part of the attack on Anaka [a village in Gulu District]. He was shot in the chest by the UPDF. He died a few days later. I gave birth to a baby boy, but he died after a month. We need to share our story if we have that opportunity. We are ready to move from one school to the other and one community to the other in Uganda for people to see hear what we have pass through and for justice should not be delay again.[5]

Arach, a 17-year-old girl from Pader district, narrated her ordeal in the hands of LRA rebels and she explained:

... Even though I am back to the school and my life is normal, I still hallucinate and dream a lot about what happened to me in the forest. I dream about my forced marriage with the Joseph Kony's commander and I was made to kill and others who were killed during our time with the LRA. ... Because of my experience, I

---

4   Interview with survivor, Pader district, December 3–21, 2012 (name changed to protect identity).

5   Interview with survivor, Pader district, December 3–21, 2012 (name changed to protect identity).

sometimes find myself shouting uncontrollably ...[6]

A 25-year-old girl Angela of Kitgum district told the author:

I was abducted and forcefully married to LRA soldier with whom I stayed with, against my will, for seven years. During this period, I underwent many abuses. ... Upon returning to my village, I was helped to trace my home within a matter of days. ... The time spent at the reception center was very short—about three days. I have heard that some other abductees underwent. ... Because of my psychological problems which relate to the painful memories of my experience.[7]

Many survivors experienced sexual violence. Another survivor, 14-year-old Atim from Gulu district, narrated to the author on how she was abducted by the LRA when she was only 8 years old. She was made to carry heavy luggage and walk for long distances inside the thick forest without food to eat and water to drink, and eventually married to a rebel. She also explained how her experience in captivity affects her today:

I was only ten years old when I gave birth to the LRA rebel's child. I was not ready to carry the pregnancy and remember very well how painful the experience, I bled a lot and feared that I would die as I just gave birth in the forest. One of the unforgettable of my experience is that I feel pain as a result of the experience. The memory of my experience has left a big mental scar on me. From time to time all this come back and haunt me. ... I feel constant pain around my waist and feel that this is as a result of the difficult childbirth that I had and a result of repeated beatings by the LRA rebels with sticks around my waist.[8]

Most survivors of sexual violence suffered during the conflict still endure the psychological effects of their experiences. These public sessions have given them an avenue to share their unforgettable experiences with the public in order to be healed.

Eunice, a 16-year-old girl of Amuru district, explained that the psychological trauma remains with her and people in the community are also not in support of her. She said:

I have a friend whose was also abducted and killed in LRA camp. Now her parent vents out her anger on me and says she wishes I was killed too because I am a ghost haunting them. ... Although it is not true, my friends tell me that because of the

---

6   Interview with survivor, Pader district, December 3–21, 2012 (name changed to protect identity).

7   Interview with survivor, Kitgum district, December 3–21, 2012 (name changed to protect identity).

8   Interview with survivor, Gulu district, December 3–21, 2012 (name changed to protect identity).

period I spent in LRA camp my behavior does not conform with that of the community again. Even my father now tells this to my mother although I am his child. ... Since God has brought me back home and given me training and showing more love to me, let me concentrate, maybe I'll do better in future. This is the only hope I have ...[9]

Jacqueline, a 20-year-old girl of Lira district who is also a survivor of abduction and forced marriage by the LRA, told the author how she would not be left at home with her relatives' children because people often think she would kill them.[10] And 22-year-old Jane of Lira district, also a survivor of LRA abduction, narrated to the author how she was rejected by her mother upon returning back to the community when her mother was traced and brought to see her at a nongovernmental organization (NGO) reception center. As a result, she has had to live at an NGO reception center since she returned 18 months ago. She "hopes that one day my mother will have a change of heart."[11]

The story of 30-year-old Kihika of Gulu district is more illustrative. She explains:

I was abducted with 7 other girls. ... All of us were about 10 to 12 years old ... and we were made

wives at a very young age. After about 4 years of life in captivity, I managed to escape and came back with 2 children and I now live with them here as a single parent. These children have difficulties. We have no money for food, school fees. ... And the culture. ... My children are treated differently, they have no clan, they don't belong. It is as if they are not meant to be ...[12]

Regarding the lack of a comprehensive reparation program targeting survivors of sexual violence, Kihika added:

What breaks me down is that we were abducted and forcefully married to LRA rebels, many of whom are now granted amnesty and resettlement packages when they return. ... Some of us women and girls that come back with children to care for are not given opportunity to share our narratives with public for next generation to learn from what they have done to us and for us to be able to receive psychological healing. The government should see that this is not fair. ... Most of us are in need of some medium to be able to share our stories. We need well organized government programme comprises of all the

9   Interview with survivor, Amuru district, December 3–21, 2012 (name changed to protect identity).

10   Interview with survivor, Lira district, December 3–21, 2012 (name changed to protect identity).

11   Interview with survivor, Lira district, December 3–21, 2012 (name changed to protect identity).

12   Interview with survivor, Gulu district, December 3–21, 2012 (name changed to protect identity).

victims and survivors of sexual violence in the camps of LRA.[13]

Many women who have been survivors of sexual violence have also been widowed. This has come with its own complications. In addition to having to cope with the consequences of the sexual violence they suffered in the hands of LRA rebels, they have to take on the role of sole family breadwinners. Nearly all survivors who were interviewed by the author expressed the need for them to narrate their ordeal with the public in an organized public program and be able to express their view in such programs. They recommended that such a program should be developed in consultation with them. The paper proposes for the creation of safe places for the staging of constructive storytelling programs where survivors of sexual violence and rape can take charge of their situation without "having to depend on the authoritative discourse of first world journalism, academic, and literature" (Caruth 2001). Given this, therefore, the following section will present the scenario of a storytelling exercise that could be organized for the healing of the survivors in Acoliland, sexually abused by the LRA.

Storytelling Intervention Program for Survivors of Sexual Violence and Rape

In the aftermath of any armed conflict or war, the social fabric of a society is often weakened, thus necessitating the need for healing and commu-nity-building activities (Dryden-Peter-son 2006). Storytelling is one medium through which individuals and communities affected by sexual violence and rape could restore hope, build resilience and confidence within and among themselves, reclaim their lives, and acknowledge trauma. Compared to other peace-building initiatives, storytelling is "an expressive medium that has few obstacles, and can be conducted regardless of economic restraints and in the dire conditions that often exist at the aftermath of war" (Ntakarutima-na 2008). In this section, a storytelling program will be designed for the healing of survivors of sexual violence and rape. This proposed program is an institution-based storytelling program involving students who are survivors of sexual violence in Acoliland.

Institution-based Storytelling Program

As mentioned above, the LRA garnered worldwide publicity and condemnation after it abducted about 139 school girls in October 10, 1996, in Aboke, northern Apac District, Uganda. One hundred and nine abducted girls escaped after series of negotiations between Sister Fassera (Principal of St. Mary's College, Aboke) and Ocaya (one of Joseph Kony's commanders) (Caruth 1993). Some of these St. Mary's College girls have told their stories at various conferences and fora around the world. This paper reckons that the women and girls' ex-

13   Interview with survivor, Gulu district, December 3–21, 2012 (name changed to protect identity).

perience of trauma and healing could be utilized in a storytelling program to encourage other young survivors of sexual violence and rape in Acoliland. This program would require the return of survivors, alongside their guardians to participate in a storytelling exercise with some selected school students and communities in all the regions of Uganda. Given that storytelling is usually conducive in protected spaces and safe environments, it would be ideal for the school program to take place in 2020 in order to give considerable time for the government in Uganda to pay attention to the plight of the Acoli people and ensure the security of Acoliland. The pilot program could be held at private or public institutions in Kampala, the capital of Uganda.

Prior to the program, it is expected that the women and girls would prepare their stories and devise a technique through which they may want to tell them. This could be through oral presentation, documentary, poetry, drama, drawing, painting, or any other medium. It is worth noting that while preparation for this program is important, storytelling does not often require intensive preparation or training. Besides the survivors of sexual violence and rape from Acoliland, I envisage that other students who are survivors of LRA abuses would participate in the program. These women and girls could be asked to share their stories alongside the other abducted women and girls that have escaped from the LRA camps. Other prospective participants in the program may include some of the parents or guardians of the

survivors, a sizeable number of teachers from schools from where students were abducted by the LRA, musicians, journalists, representatives of civil society groups, psychologists or counselors, health workers, community council chiefs, and clerics.

The program, which is not expected to require expensive facilities or resources, could be financed by the Ugandan government, NGOs, and humanitarian agencies working in the area of sexual violence prevention and healing. The equipment and resources to be used at the program may include: a hall, a projector, a sound system, computer, school bus, a first aid kit, chairs, tables, food, and drinks. The program's proceedings could begin with a prayer session led by a cleric. Afterward, a minute or two should be dedicated for quiet reflection. After the prayer session, there should be a short briefing to reiterate the purpose of the storytelling program. This could be done by one of the chiefs or teachers in attendance. The briefing should underscore the relevance of the storytelling exercise in terms of its potential to foster solidarity, healing, as well as creating the opportunity for survivors of sexual violence and rape to express themselves. The briefing is to be followed by the storytelling exercise beginning with the stories of the representatives of survivors in Acoliland.

It is hoped that the girls' stories of courage, persistence, faith, and resilience will instill confidence and hope in the minds and hearts of the audience. When all the representatives of survivors of sexual violence must have shared their stories, the chairman of the program may invite the audience to engage them by acknowledging and expressing some words of gratitude. The audience may also validate the girls or offer some words of support and encouragement. The attendees could also be asked to share what lessons they might have learned from the representatives of survivors' stories of trauma, agency, and resilience. As stated, there is always the possibility of blame allocation or re-traumatization to occur during such an exercise. To avoid or manage such an outcome, survivors should be adequately prepped prior to the program to understand that the program is an opportunity to restore hope and build agency and resilience. Even so, such preparation may not necessarily prevent tension and conflict from occurring. If tension arises, the musicians at the program could step in to perform some music and invite the attendees to join in. Such musical performance has the potential of dousing and easing any tension that may arise during the program.

The services of the psychologist and health worker may be needed should survivors of sexual violence and rape become emotionally exhausted or re-traumatized. At the end of the exercise, the safety of the attendees and the safe return to their respective communities must be guaranteed. With the consent of the storytellers, the documented stories of the survivors of sexual violence and rape may be stored in the form of a video documentary. This could form part of a new curriculum for peace education in institutions in Uganda. A year after the pilot program, a follow-up evaluation should be conducted to determine the impact of the program. If the program is judged to be successful, it could be replicated in several regions of Uganda where there are many survivors of sexual violence and rape of the LRA. In telling their stories, the survivors of sexual violence and rape are providing a "better story" that is more acceptable to their colleagues and communities than the brainwashing narratives of the LRA rebels. Storytelling, especially in the context of armed conflict and violence, also opens the discussion on what is right and wrong and challenges individuals to reconsider their values and beliefs that may be detrimental to their well-being and the stability of their society. The stories of the students can also play an important role in peace education and empowering young women and girls to be peacemakers.

Conclusion

I have, in this paper, examined the potential role of storytelling in the healing of survivors of sexual violence and rape in Acoliland. Having defined and conceptualized the notions of survivors of sexual violence and rape and storytelling, I have presented some stories of survivors of sexual violence and rape. Thereafter, a potential storytelling program was designed and examined: an institution-based storytelling program involving students who are survivors of sexual violence in Acoliland and who have been directly or indirectly affected by the sexual violence and rape by the LRA. The paper underscored the need for the Acoliland girls studying in other regions of the world and other students in Uganda who have shown remarkable courage and resilience in spite of or because of their victimization by the LRA to share their stories at the institution-based storytelling program. I argued that the stories by the survivors of sexual violence and rape can serve as a source of courage to others, and that if documented and stored, they may also serve as a teaching tool for peace-building in Uganda and other countries in Africa. I have also argued that through the act of telling their stories, the survivors of sexual violence and rape trauma are acknowledged, leading to the restoration of trust, agency, and hope. In the final analysis, it is worth noting that storytelling is not a guaranteed strategy for the healing of survivors of sexual violence and rape. It is proposed in this paper as one medium through which survivors of sexual violence and rape can acknowledge and own their trauma, take charge of their lives, and transform their societies. For storytelling to be an effective healing exercise, other aspects of healing such as counseling, healthcare, and social assistance should be made available to the survivors of sexual violence and rape.

References

Akumu, C., I. Amony, and G. Otim. 2005. "Suffering in Silence: A Study of Sexual and Gender Based Violence (SGBV) in Pabbo Camp, Gulu District, Northern Uganda." *Gulu District Sub Working Group on SGBV*.

Barton, B., and D. Booth. 2000. *Storyworks: How Teachers Can Use Shared Stories in the New Curriculum*. Markham, ON: Pembroke Publishers.

Behrend, H. 1998. "The Holy Spirit Movements New World: Discourse and Development in the North of Uganda." In *Developing Uganda*, edited by H. B. Hansen and M. Twaddle. USA, Ohio University Press/Oxford, UK: James Currey.

Brison, J. S. 2002. *Aftermath: Violence and the Remaking of a Self*, 51–54. Princeton, NJ: Princeton University Press.

Burk, N. M. 1997. "Using Personal Narratives as a Pedagogical Tool: Empowering Students Through Stories." Paper presented at the *Annual Meeting of the National Communication Association 83rd*, 1–10, Chicago, IL, November 19–23.

Caruth, C. 1993. "Violence and Time: Traumatic Survivals." *Assemblage* 20: 24–25.

Caruth, C. 2001. "Parting Words: Trauma, Silence and Survival." *Cultural Values* 5 (1): 7–26.

Chaitin, J. 2003. "Stories, Narratives, and Storytelling." In *Beyond Intractability, Conflict Research Consortium*, edited by Guy Burgess and Heidi Burgess. Boulder, CO: University of Colorado Press.

Daemmrich, I. G. 2003. "Paradise and Storytelling: Interconnecting Gender, Motif, and Narrative Structure." *Narrative Journal* 11 (2): 213–233. doi:10.1353/nar.2003.0006.

Dolan, C. 2011. *Social Torture: The Case of Northern Uganda 1986–2006*, 1–338. London: Berghahn Books.

Dryden-Peterson, S. 2006. "'I Find Myself as Someone Who is in the Forest': Urban Refugees as Agents of Social Change in Kampala, Uganda." *Journal of Refugee Studies* 19 (3): 381–393.

Dyson, A. H., and C. Genishi. 1994. "Introduction: The Need for Story." In *The Need for Story: Cultural Diversity in Classroom and Community*, edited by. A. H. Dyson and C. Genishi, 1–7. Urbana, IL: National Council of Teachers of English.

Goodman, A. "Storytelling for Good Causes." *Stanford Centre for Business Management*. Podcast retrieved October 17, 2015 from iTunes, April 22, 2008.

Herman, J. 1997. *Trauma and Recovery: The Aftermath of Violence—from Domestic Abuse to Political Terror*, 1, Reprint edition. Basic Books.

Hilder, M. B. 2005. "The Enemy's Gospel: Deconstructing Exclusivity and Inventing Inclusivity Through the Power of Story." *Journal of Curriculum and Supervision* 20 (2): 158–181, 167.

Human Rights Watch. 2003. *Abducted and Abused: Renewed Conflict in Northern Uganda; Uganda Child Abductions Skyrocket in the North; Uganda: Stolen Children Abduction and Recruitment in Northern Uganda*. New York: Human Rights Watch.

Hutchinson, A. 1999. *Students on the Margins: Education, Stories, Dignity*, 85–93. Albany, NY: State University of New York Press.

King, T. 2003. *The Truth about Stories: A Native Narrative*. Toronto, ON: House of Anansi Press.

Miller, E. 1996. "Visuals Accompanying Face-to-face Storytelling." Unpublished MA Thesis, New York University. Accessed 15 December 2013. http://www.storytellingandvideoconferencing.com/15.html.

Nicholson, D., and L. Nicholson. 2005. "Caring to Question: Some Ethical Dimensions to Storytelling in Practice." *The Early Childhood Educator* 20 (5): 23–25.

Ntakarutimana, E. 2008. "The Challenge of Recovering from War Trauma in the African Great Lakes Region: An Experience from Centre Ubuntu in the Project Colombe Network." *Intervention* 6 (2): 162–166.

Odongo, O. 2003. "Causes of Armed Conflicts in Uganda." *Historical Memory Synthetic Paper, Centre for Basic Research (CBR) Conference*, Hotel Africana, Historical Memory Project Synthetic Writings.

Okello, C. M., and L. Hovil. 2007. "Confronting the Reality of Gender-based Violence in Northern Uganda." *International Journal of Transitional Justice* 1 (1): 433–443.

Simmons, A. 2006. *What is Story? Story Factor: Inspiration, Influence, and Persuasion Through the Art of Storytelling.* New York: Basic Books.

Sogol, W. 2014. *"A Word's Worth: How Storytelling Can Help the World Achieve Gender Equity."* New York, NY: Women Deliver. Accessed 23 December 2014. http://www.womendeliver. org/updates/entry/a-words-worth-how-storytellingcan-help-the-world-achieve-gender-equity.

UNHCR. 2003. "Sexual and Gender-Based Violence Against Refugees, Returnees and Internally Displaced Persons." *Guidelines for Prevention and Response,* UNHCR.

United Nations Children's Fund (UNICEF). 2012. *UN Joint Programme on Gender-Based Violence Programme Document.* Kampala, Uganda: UNICEF.

United Nations, Declaration on the Elimination of Violence against Women: General Assembly Resolution 48/104 of December 20, 1993 (A/RES/48/104). Article 1.

Watts, I. N. 1992. *Making Stories.* Portsmouth, NH: Heinemann.

Watts, C., and C. Zimmerman. 2002. "Violence Against Women: Global Scope and Magnitude." *The Lancet* 359 (9313): 1232–1237.

LGBT Identity: The Illustration of "Othering" in India[1]

Kunal Debnath

Assistant Professor, Department of Political Science,
Kazi Nazrul University

ABSTRACT

"Social identities are relational; groups typically define themselves in relation to others. This is because identity has little meaning without the 'other'" (Okolie 2003). So, can we ignore the "other" identity to examine the concept of identity as a whole? "Other" is the counterpart of "self," and means those who are neglected and situated at the margin of the power structure. These concepts of "other" and "self" have been popularized after the emergence of postmodernism and postcolonialism. The lesbian, gay, bisexual and transgender (LGBT) community can be regarded as "other" of the male–female binary. The state has a big role to create and/or erase the differentiation between "self" and "other." The demand of the LGBT community, that is, the exclusion of Section 377 from the Indian Penal Code is yet to be fulfilled by the Indian State, "but it also made possible the formation of a 'reverse' discourse: homosexuality began to speak in its own behalf, to demand its legitimacy" (Foucault 1976, 101). The aims of my paper are to find out the theoretical aspects of the otherness in the case of LGBT. What should be the way of inclusion of the LGBT community in the mainstream?

Key words: Other; Self; Power; LGBT; Identity; Homosexuality; Heterosexuality; Democracy.

---

1   Earlier version of this paper was presented in ICSSR Funded National Seminar on "Identity and Security in India in the Era of Globalization" organized by the Department of Political Science, The University of Burdwan, W.B. India on 17th and 18th March, 2016.

I would like to convey my gratitude to my family members, teachers, and colleagues for stimulating me and helping me as well. Besides said individuals, I would like to express thanks to all the scholars who appeared in the reference section. Special thanks to the anonymous reviewers for their constructive suggestions and pieces of advice.

摘要

"各种社会认同相互联系；各团体对自身的定义都和其他团体相关。这是因为认同在没有'他者'的情况下便失去意义"(Okolie 2003)。那么，我们能否在抛开"他者"认同的情况下检测认同这一整个概念？"他者"是"自我"的对立面，它意味着人们被忽视，被位于权力结构的边缘。"他者"和"自我"的概念在后现代主义和后殖民主义出现后开始流行起来。女同性恋者，男同性恋者，双性恋者和变性者（简称LGBT）社区可以被视作"男女二元"（male-female binary）的他者。国家在建立或消除"自我"和"他者"之间的差别上需要发挥重要作用。LGBT社区的需求—从印度刑事法典中废除第377条—还需要印度本国执行，"但同时也可能形成'相反'的论述"：同性恋者开始代表自身发言，要求其"合法权利"(Foucault 1976, 101)。本文的目的是发现LGBT案例中关于"他者"的理论依据。LGBT社区在主流社会中应该以何种方式被接纳？

关键词：他者；自我；权力；LGBT；认同；同性恋；异性恋；民主

Resumen

La identidad social es relacional: típicamente, cada grupo se define en relación a los otros. Esto se debe a que la identidad no tiene sentido sin el "Otro" (Okolie 2003). Por ende, ¿podemos ignorar la identidad del "Otro" para examinar el concepto de identidad holísticamente? El "Otro" es la contraparte del "yo", significando aquellos que son excluidos y situados al margen de las estructuras de poder. Este concepto del "Otro" y del "yo" se ha popularizado después del surgimiento del posmodernismo y el poscolonialismo. La comunidad lésbica, gay, bisexual y transgénero (LGBT) puede ser entendida como el "Otro" en el binario masculino-femenino. El estado cumple un papel importante en la creación y/o destrucción de la diferencia entre el "yo" y el "otro". La denuncia de la comunidad LGBT, es decir, la exclusión de la Sección 377 del Código Penal Indio todavía no ha sido realizada por parte del estado indio, "pero hizo posible la formación de un discurso "invertido": la homosexualidad empieza a hablar por sí misma, a exigir su legitimidad" (Foucault 1976, 101). El propósito de mi artículo es indagar acerca de los aspectos teóricos de la otredad en el caso de la comunidad LGBT. ¿Cuál debería ser el modo de inclusión de la comunidad LGBT en la cultura mayoritaria?

Palabras clave: *"Otro", "Yo", Poder, LGBT, Identidad, Homosexuali-*
dad, Heterosexualidad, Democracia.

Introduction

From time immemorial, a person or a group has had an inevitable concern about his/her or its identity. Identity is the cornerstone of all societies and it comprises the culture, beliefs, psychological orientation, proneness, affinity et cetera. Identity is one of the key variables in a society that makes differences among people or groups. Nowadays, we are heading towards a world with an identity crisis because "in a liquid modern setting of life, identities are perhaps the most common, most acute, most deeply felt and troublesome incarnations of ambivalence" (Bauman 2004). Moreover, "social identities are relational; groups typically define themselves in relation to others. This is because identity has little meaning without the 'other'" (Okolie 2003). So, can we ignore the "other" identity to examine the concept of identity as a whole! "Other" is the counterpart of "self", meaning those who are ignored and situated at the margin or periphery of the power structure. The creation of otherness (also called *othering*) happens only when individuals are classified into two categorical groups: them and us, "them" referring to the "other" and "us" referring to the "self". The out-group or "other" is a result of its opposition to the in-group or "self"

and its lack of identity (Staszak 2009). Thus, social othering happens when one group excludes another from society in terms of their identity. So, otherness or othering is a consequence of social exclusion. It is not a new phenomenon because since bygone days

> social exclusion has remained associated with what may be called social othering, a process of labelling and branding some groups of people as the 'other', meaning abject and 'barbarian', 'traditional', 'primitive' and so on. The European Enlightenment and its offshoot, modernity, could not do away with this dichotomization of the 'we' and the 'other' ... (Bhattacharyya, Sarkar, and Kar 2010, 4)

In point of fact, identity as an "Other" and "Otherness" of "other" is, perhaps, inevitable in all societies at all times, but the concept of "other" has been popularized after the emergence of postmodernism and postcolonialism since postmodernism exhibited how discourses of power define people and impute a particular identity, and "postcolonialism claims the rights of all people on the earth to the same material and cultural well-being" (Young 2003, 2).

Key Concepts and Definitions

The term "queer" is very relevant in this connection. Queer means odd or deviating from the usual or expected. Queer denotes those who are practicing homosexuality or lesbianism or bisexuality, and it is against the "normal" mode of heterosexuality (Menon 2005). So, the term queer is often used for describing homosexual people or the LGBT (Lesbian, Gay, Bisexual, and Transgender) community; in other words, queer is an offensive term used for homosexual people or the LGBT community. However, LGBT does not represent only homosexual people, rather it is an umbrella term that encompasses many categories, viz. lesbian, gay, bisexual, transgender and, most importantly, transsexual and intersexual nature. Before explaining different types under the umbrella term LGBT, it would be better to explain first the differences between sex and gender.

Sex is biological in nature, unalterable and based on the natural inequalities (man and women), whereas gender is a socially constructed idea, alterable and based on the conventional inequalities (masculine and feminine). Sex is related to biological nature; on the other hand, gender is related to behavior, activities and the entire culture, so to say, determined by the society. Lesbian, gay and bisexual people are clearly concerned with their sexuality—lesbian means a female who is sexually attracted to another female, or a homosexual female; gay refers to a male who is sexually attracted to another male, or a homosexual male; and the term bisex-

ual refers to those persons who are attracted to both males and females. Now the differences between transsexual and transgender ought to be explained. People who are transsexual feel emotionally and psychologically that they were born with a wrong sex. Their assigned sexual identity is not the same with their sexual desire or orientation. They intend to go for surgery and/or sex reassignment therapy for satiating their sexual needs. On the other side, transgender is a multifaceted term, usually referring to a person who feels that his/her gender behavior, culture or outfit in reference to sex is not conforming to his/her masculine/feminine gender identity prescribed by the society concerned. Transgender people, unlike transsexual, do not intend to alter their sex by surgery and/or sex reassignment therapy. Another category of the LGBT umbrella community is intersex, which denotes those who do not fit with male or female in terms of reproductive organs. Moreover, transgender, transsexual and intersex people are considered the third gender or third sex. Thus, LGBT people are the "other" of the male–female sexual and masculine–feminine gender binary.

In this way, "by limiting gender to simply the definitions of 'man' and 'woman,' there is a wide range of identities that are excluded from the equation" (Basiliere 2011, 142). However, as stated earlier, LGBT people are labeled as queer for their deviant nature of sexual and gender identity. But, now the question is, why are the LGBT people queer? Merely because their sexual identity and/or gender identity is not analogous with that of the majority of people of the human society? Because mental, physical, and psychological desires of LGBT people are not akin with those of the majority of people? Because their sexuality is not productive? Because LGBT "queer" people are positioned outside the mainstream, and not centered in the decision-making power structure?

Probably, all answers would be yes in this discourse. Apropos of the term "discourse" it should be noted that Foucault contributed a significant notion about the relation between discourse and power. Discourse means an influential statement to define something, describe something and narrate something. Power has a key role to construct a particular discourse. So a reason or rationality is always set up by the discourses of power. Some people always intend to standardize their discourse and exclude the rest who are the deviant from "their" reason or rationality or stand, and produce "the other". Thus, the Foucauldian notion of power and discourse unveils the way how discourses of power are exercised in all societies to marginalize the "deviant" people or groups. At that juncture, homosexuality, perhaps, has to create a reverse discourse to be "the self", to be "centered". Foucault had a credence about the reverse discourse of homosexuality: "... it also made possible the formation of a 'reverse' discourse: homosexuality began to speak in its own behalf, to demand that its legitimacy or 'naturality' be acknowledged ..." (Foucault 1976, 101).

Here, two concepts can be introduced which are closely linked with the LGBT queer identity—heteronormativity and homonormativity. Heteronormativity stands for normal and preferred sexual orientation, like sexual relation ought to be made between male and female. Homonormativity is a reverse conception of heteronormativity because it is in favor of homosexuality. However, homonormativity does not promote homosexuality as the only preferred sexual orientation. Homonormativity is "a politics that does not contest dominant heteronormative assumptions and institutions, but upholds and sustains them, while promising the possibility of a demobilized gay constituency and a privatized, depoliticized gay culture anchored in domesticity and consumption" (Duggan 2002). But, importantly, demands of all the constituent members of the LGBT community are not identical. For instance, lesbian or gay people are demanding same-sex marriage or the right to homosexuality, but not all lesbians or gays are in favor of same-sex marriage; some of this section argues for legalization of same-sex marriage and some are against the legalization of same-sex marriage (Reczek and Rothblum 2012). Bisexual people are concerned about both homosexuality and heterosexuality. Lesbian, gay and bisexual people are looking for that time when homosexuality would be treated by the state as a human right. On the other hand, transgender people are demanding their civil rights, like social and economic security, abolition of discrimination they have been facing since antiquity, reservation in terms of education and job et cetera; political rights, like the right to elect and the right to be elected. Most of the lesbian, gay and bisexual people belong to the higher class of the society. They are well established in terms of their livelihood. On the other hand, transgender people are, mostly, from the downtrodden section of society. They struggle for their livelihood. Thus, the LGBT community is not monolithic in nature.

LGBT Issues in India

In ancient India, there were a few examples of LGBT-related issues. Here, we can consider the example of *Shikhandi* of the *Mahabharata*. *Shikhandi* was born as a female named *Shikhandini* and transformed her sex from female to male, but as an impotent person, and became a transsexual. It is described in the *Vedas*, *Kama Sutra* and many ancient Indian scriptures that there were three types of human nature or *prakriti* in ancient India. These are *Pums Prakriti* (male nature), *Stri Prakriti* (female nature) and *Tritiya Prakriti* (third nature). Here, *prakriti* refers to both sexual and gender identity together. The people of *tritiya prakriti* were entitled to their basic rights. They were endorsed to keep their own societies and permitted to live together by marriage and engage in all means of occupation (Wilhelm 2010, 16–17). Provenance of three types of gender is described in the foundation of Hindu law *Manusmriti*: "A male child is produced by a greater quantity of male seed, a female child by the prevalence of the female; if (both are) equal, a hermaph-

rodite or a boy and a girl ..." (The Laws of Manu, III, 49). Thus, ancient Vedic India and Hinduism acknowledged the third sex and also homosexuality, and was more open-minded than modern India regarding sanctioning rights to the third gender community and homosexuality, but interestingly, it did not sanction frivolous sexual behavior and promiscuousness:

Sometimes people misunderstand that, by accepting the existence of a third gender, Hinduism was therefore sanctioning loose sexual behavior or promiscuity. This is not the case, however. Accepting homosexual as a social class is not about their sexual behaviors—that will vary from person to person. Homosexual people can be celibate, monogamous, or promiscuous, just as heterosexual can be celibate, monogamous, or promiscuous. In Vedic society, many gay people lived in complete celibacy and served as a temple priests. At the same time, homosexual couples were known to marry "with complete faith in one another" as mentioned in the *Kama Sutra* ... (Wilhelm 2010, 12).

Homonormativity, heteronormativity and the queer identity of the LGBT community, which made them "other", all are consequences of European modernity and derived from European colonialism in India. The process of othering of the LGBT community has been institutionalized and legitimized by section 377 of the Indian Penal Code (henceforth referred to as IPC) introduced in 1860 by the then British colonial masters. According to section 377 of the IPC, "Unnatural offences—Whoever voluntarily has carnal intercourse 'against the order of nature' with any man, woman or animal, shall be punished with imprisonment for life, or with imprisonment of either description for a term which may extend to ten years, and shall also be liable to fine. Explanation—Penetration is sufficient to constitute the carnal intercourse necessary to the offence described in this section." By this very section of the IPC, homosexuality is "against the order of nature"; that is why it is illicit as well as a punishable offence. In India, the LGBT community tried to establish homonormativity through the judicial mechanism.

In 2001, the Naz Foundation, an NGO working for the welfare and rehabilitation of people with HIV, filed a Public Interest Litigation (PIL) against National Capital Territory of Delhi (Naz Foundation vs. Govt. of NCT of Delhi, WP [Civil] No. 7455 of 2001) at the Delhi High Court challenging section 377 of the IPC. Later in 2006, the Naz Foundation filed a special leave petition before the Supreme Court of India demanding decriminalization of homosexuality by repealing section 377 of the IPC. Significantly, the Delhi High Court gave a verdict stating some portions of this particular section of the IPC are *ultra vires* in nature and violated the fundamental rights mentioned in the Indian Constitution. A number of appeals were filed at the Supreme

Court of India against the verdict of the Delhi High Court. Then, in 2012, the Ministry of Home Affairs gave a note of dissent to the Supreme Court about the Delhi High Court's verdict, but later, surprisingly, the Central Government changed its stand on the said issue and supported decriminalization of homosexuality. The Central Government has been reprimanded by the apex court for its capricious attitude. Finally, in December 2013, the Supreme Court of India set aside the Delhi High Court's verdict. The apex court observed that the Parliament should debate and decide later in this regard. Recently, the Madras High Court has asked the center "When more than 30 countries, including a conservative nation like Ireland, have decriminalized homosexuality and legalized gay marriage by way of referendum, getting 62.07% votes in favor, why not India decriminalize homosexuality?" (*Times of India*, January 31, 2016).

On February 2, 2016 the Supreme Court of India said that it will review this colonial-era law regarding homosexuality. Hence, even after many tug of wars in the Delhi High Court and the Supreme Court of India, section 377 of the IPC is continuing with unabated strength. The irony is that homosexuality has already been decriminalized in England by the "Sexual Offences Act 1967" but the same is "against the order of nature" and criminal offence in India by the section of IPC made by the colonial British rulers. Besides these legal steps, the LGBT queer people have been demanding their rights in a diverse manner, supported by different sections of society. Several gay "pride parades" have been organized in several cities, like Bengaluru, Delhi, Indore, Kolkata, Puducherry, Bhubaneswar and Chennai. These pride parades received huge support from the common people, media, celebrities et cetera. One LGBT magazine and one gay magazine, namely "Pink Pages" and "Bombay Dost" have been published since 2009. Some LGBT films have been exhibited in the Mumbai Pride festivals in 2010 and 2011. In Madurai the first LGBT Queer Rainbow Festival was held in 2012 with the demand to eradicate social discriminations faced by the LGBT people. In recent times, the LGBT movement, one variant of New Social Movements, led by "homoprotectionist" people have gained the attention of the intelligentsia from India and abroad. After the 2013 verdict of the apex court of India, the LGBT community started to protest more in a systematic way by organizing several Pride Parades. In this way, they have been able to garner the support of some celebrities, the media and the common people. These legal and social initiatives taken by the LGBT people along with supporters substantiated the observation "where there is power, there is resistance" (Foucault 1976, 95). This is, undoubtedly, an endeavor to establish a "counter-hegemony" by homonormativity against hegemonic heteronormativity.

Though in many Western countries the right to homosexuality has been granted to the LGBT "Queer" people as a human right and the U.S.A. has established herself as a global defender of LGBT "Queer" rights by giving these rights as human rights, these examples are still a mirage elsewhere. For example, we notice the homophobic or heterocentric attitude of postcolonial India, though there is a long tradition of democracy. Globally, in more than 70 countries resembling India, homosexuality is considered a crime. Some of these countries impose fine or imprisonment like India (United Nations News Centre 2010). Notwithstanding, the United Nations is in favor of decriminalization of homosexuality all over the world and this standpoint was legitimized by the statement of Ban Ki-moon, the Secretary-General of the UNO:

> Together, we seek the repeal of laws that criminalize homosexuality, that permit discrimination on the basis of sexual orientation or gender identity, that encourage violence. When individuals are attacked, abused or imprisoned because of their sexual orientation, we must speak out. We cannot stand by. We cannot be silent. (United Nations News Centre 2010)

Even in article 16 (1) of United Nations Universal Declaration of Human Rights stated that:

> Men and women of full age, without any limitation due to race, nationality or religion, have the right to marry and to found a family. They are entitled to equal rights as to marriage, during marriage and at its dissolution. (United Nations Organization 1948)

On LGBT Identity in India

Now, the question is what should be the way(s) or method(s) regarding the dissolution of social as well as institutional othering of the LGBT community to the mainstream Indian society. Could the two strategies, expounded by Claude Levi-Strauss, namely *anthropoemic* and *anthropophagic*, be employed for annihilating the otherness of the LGBT community? The *anthropoemic* strategy involves rejecting, vomiting and incarcerating, and the other strategy, *anthropophagic* involves "devouring" and "digesting" the stranger.

> The first strategy consists in 'vomiting', spitting out the others seen as incurably strange and alien, barring physical contact, dialogue, social intercourse and all varieties of *commercium*, commensality or *connubium*. The extreme variants of the 'emic' strategy are now, as always, incarceration, deportation and murder. The upgraded, 're-fined' (modernized) forms of the 'emic' strategy are spatial separation, urban ghettos, and selective access to spaces and selective barring of their use. The second strategy consists in a soi-disant 'disalienation' of alien substances: 'ingesting', 'devouring' foreign bodies and spirits so that they may be made, through metabolism, identical with, and no longer distinguishable from, the 'ingesting' body. This strategy took

an equally wide range of forms: from cannibalism to enforced assimilation—cultural crusades, wars of attrition declared on local customs, calendars, cults, dialects, and other 'prejudices' and 'superstitions'. If the first strategy was aimed at the exile or annihilation of *the others*, the second was aimed at the suspension or annihilation of their *otherness*. (Bauman 2000, 101)

Neither the *anthropoemic* method nor the *anthropophagic* method is adequate for this case because, according to Bauman, neither of these are working properly in a globalizing world. Rather, since India has a long tradition of democracy, this problem can be solved through democracy because "democracy is nothing if it is not inclusionary" [and] "the removal of social exclusion remains thus at the top of the agenda of the advocates of inclusionary, democratic society" (Bhattacharyya, Sarkar, and Kar 2010, 1). Liberal states, however, are not beyond question since the liberal discourse is deep-rooted in the sovereign authority of the individuals over their socio-political rights, right to property and right to freedom. LGBT queer people are not entitled to enjoy these rights. This indicates the limits of the liberal democratic state. If the liberal democratic state does not ensure the demands of the "other", then the liberal democracy turns into what J.S. Mill described as "tyranny of the majority". In fact, all "so-called" egalitarian, libertarian and utilitarian states have failed to accept "otherness".

However, considering "tyranny of the majority" in a liberal representative democratic state, the rights of the minority as well as "other" may be protected by defining some rights as "fundamental rights" in order that these rights could not be breached by the representatives, even by the majority of the representatives. Now questions might arise as to which rights are to be incorporated into fundamental rights and which not to, and/or how the existing gestalt of "fundamental rights" are to be changed. Incorporating new rights into fundamental rights or changing the existing structure of fundamental rights may be possible through reasonable deliberations and arguments, among various opinions, in a democratic process (Chatterjee 2000, 47–52). Hence, the state has to take initiatives to empower the LGBT section in all spheres viz. constitutional safeguards regarding special provisions to people of the third gender and third sex. Also, initiatives should be taken by the Parliament for repealing section 377 from the IPC. Though, in a significant judgment on April 15, 2014, the Supreme Court of India has directed the center and the states to recognize transgender people as a third gender as well as being socially and educationally backward. Moreover, the Supreme Court has directed the government to ensure reservation for their admission in educational institutions and public appointments. Recently in a hearing on June 30, 2016, the Supreme Court of India clarified that lesbian, gay and bisexual people should not be included in the category of transgen-

ders. This is, however, not an adequate measure because not only "affirmative actions", in terms of reservation, financial aids et cetera, but also some other needful actions need to be taken for the whole LGBT community, not just for the transgender section. The LGBT people should be included in the decision-making process of the state, since every section of a society has similar rights to engage themselves, either directly or indirectly, with the policy-framing and policy-implementing process in a democratic state. Here, an example can be given of the British Parliament: in 2016 there are 35 MPs in the UK Parliament from the LGBT community (Hooper 2016).

Conclusion

Once upon a time, indigenous Indian culture was usurped by the British colonial culture. Now the time has come to follow either the ancient Indian attitude or the postmodern Western attitude toward the LGBT community. Postcolonialism always advocates against marginality and marginalization; always stands in favor of the rights of the subaltern. Thus, it is indeed a tragedy of postcolonial India that she has still remained unable to annihilate marginality and marginalization. If the state strictly adheres to the colonial stands regarding the LGBT question, then it would be more painful to the LGBT community. As is already known, however, power is not exercised only in the domain of the state, rather power relations exist everywhere. Therefore, breaches of rights happen extensively in the domain of Indian society. Hence, only affirmative action, right to education, health support, repeal of section 377 from the IPC, right to elect and to be elected, and fundamental rights are not adequate measures for inclusion of the LGBT people, because these have not ensured the inclusion of the entire LGBT section people in the domain of the society. These measures, except repeal of section 377 from the IPC, might be helpful to the people of the third gender or third sex, but not to the lesbian, gay and bisexual people. In addition to the aforesaid measures, a change of approach toward the LGBT people is needed all the more. Social appointments of the LGBT people, social communication, reciprocity, exchange of feelings with the LGBT people are more important for social inclusion of the LGBT people. In other words, neither the *anthropoemic* nor the *anthropophagic* method proposed by Claude Levi-Strauss, but rather initiatives for comprehending the otherness of the LGBT people need to be taken. Social inclusion does not mean only inclusion in a substantive level, but also in the procedural level. In the era of globalization, multiculturalism and the neo-liberal regime, it should be accepted that all are "free to choose" their culture according to their needs and choices. So, the society has to be more inclusive, more accommodative and more assimilative.

References

Basiliere, Jenna. 2011. "Outside the Binary: Transgendered Politics on a Global Stage." In *The Politics of Inclusion and Exclusion: Identity Politics in Twenty-First Century America*, edited by David F. Ericson, 137–150. New York: Routledge.

Bauman, Zygmunt. 2000. *Liquid Modernity*. Cambridge: Polity Press.

Bauman, Zygmunt. 2004. *Identity: Conversasions with Bendetto Vecchi*. Cambridge: Polity Press.

Bhattacharyya, Harihar, Partha Sarkar, and Angshuman Kar. 2010. "Introduction: The Politics of Social Exclusion in India: Democracy at the Crossroads." In *The Politics of Social Exclusion in India: Democracy at the Crossroads*, edited by Harihar Bhattacharyya, Partha Sarkar, and Angshuman Kar, 1–13. Oxon: Routledge.

Chatterjee, Partha. 2000. *Itihaser Uttaridhikar*. Kolkata: Ananda.

Duggan, Lisa. 2002. "The New Homonormativity: The Sexual Politics of Neoliberalism." In *Materializing Democracy: Toward a Revitalized Cultural Politics*, edited by Russ Castronovo and Dana D. Nelson, 175–194. Durham, NC: Duke University Press.

Foucault, Michel. 1976. *History of the Sexuality, Volume I: An Introduction*. New York: Pantheon Books.

Hooper, Matt. 2016. "The UK has More LGBT MPs Than Anywhere Else in the World." *Gay Times*, February 21. Accessed 9 March 2016. https://www.gaytimes.co.uk/news/28378/the-uk-has-more-lgbt-mps-than-anywhere-else-in-the-world/.

Menon, Nivedita. 2005. "How Natural is Normal? Feminism and Compulsory Heterosexuality." In *Because I have a Voice: Queer Politics in India*, edited by Arvind Narrain and Gautam Bhan, 33–40. New Delhi: Yoda Press.

Okolie, Andrew. 2003. "Introduction to the Special Issue—Identity: Now You Don't See It; Now You Do." *Identity: An International Journal of Theory and Research* (Routledge) 3 (1): 1–7. Accessed 5 January 2016. http://www.tandfonline.com/doi/abs/10.1207/S1532706XID0301_01?tab=permissions&scroll=top.

Reczek, Corinne, and Esther Rothblum. 2012. "A Little Bit Pregnant? The Ethics of Same-Sex Marriage." In *Handbook of LGBT-Affirmative Couple and Family Therapy*, edited by Jerry J Bigner and Joseph L Wetchler, 459-473. New York: Routledge.

Staszak, Jean-Francois. 2009. *Other/Otherness*. Vol. 8, in *International Encyclopeadia of Human Geography*, edited by R. Kitchin and N. Thrift, 43–47. Oxford: Elsevier.

The Laws of Manu. Accessed 4 March 2016. http://www.sacred-texts.com/hin/manu/manu03.htm.

Times of India. 2016. "Shouldn't LGBT People's Rights and Privacy be Protected, Madras HC Asks Centre." *Times of India*, January 31. Accessed 2 February 2016. http://timesofindia.indiatimes.com/india/Shouldnt-LGBT-peoples-rights-and-privacy-be-protected-Madras-HC-asks-Centre/articleshow/50795376.cms.

Times of India. 2016. "Supreme Court Will Review Law Criminalizing Homosexuality." *Times of India*, February 2. Accessed 2 February 2016. http://timesofindia.indiatimes.com/india/Supreme-Court-will-review-law-criminalizing-homosexuality/articleshow/50823515.cms.

United Nations News Centre. 2010. "Universal Decriminalization of Homosexuality a Human Rights Imperative—Ban." *UN News Centre*, December 10. Accessed 6 March 2016. http://www.un.org/apps/news/story.asp?NewsID=37026#.Vtxu9Ob1Ru4.

United Nations Organization. 1948. *Universal Declaration of Human Rights*. Accessed 7 March 2016. http://www.ohchr.org/EN/UDHR/Documents/UDHR_Translations/eng.pdf.

Wilhelm, A. D. 2010. *Tritiya-Prakriti: People of the Third Sex* (Abridged Version). Philadelphia: Xlibris Corporation.

Young, Robert J.C. 2003. *Postcolonialism: A Very Short Introduction*. New York: Oxford University Press.

www.ingramcontent.com/pod-product-compliance
Lightning Source LLC
Chambersburg PA
CBHW081648270326
41933CB00018B/3390